822.33
S100g
Ghose, Zulfikar,
Shakespeare's
mortal knowledge

SHAKESPEARE'S MORTAL KNOWLEDGE

Also by Zulfikar Ghose

Criticism

HAMLET, PRUFROCK AND LANGUAGE
THE FICTION OF REALITY
THE ART OF CREATING FICTION

Poetry

THE LOSS OF INDIA
JETS FROM ORANGE
THE VIOLENT WEST
A MEMORY OF ASIA
SELECTED POEMS

Fiction

THE CONTRADICTIONS
THE MURDER OF AZIZ KHAN
THE INCREDIBLE BRAZILIAN: THE NATIVE
THE BEAUTIFUL EMPIRE
A DIFFERENT WORLD
CRUMP'S TERMS
HULME'S INVESTIGATIONS INTO THE BOGART SCRIPT
A NEW HISTORY OF TORMENTS
DON BUENO
FIGURES OF ENCHANTMENT
THE TRIPLE MIRROR OF THE SELF

Autobiography

CONFESSIONS OF A NATIVE-ALIEN

Shakespeare's Mortal Knowledge

A Reading of the Tragedies

Zulfikar Ghose
Professor of English
The University of Texas at Austin

St. Martin's Press New York

First published in the United States of America in 1993

Printed in Hong Kong

ISBN 0–312–08545–1

Library of Congress Cataloging-in-Publication Data
Ghose, Zulfikar, 1935–
Shakespeare's mortal knowledge : a reading of the tragedies / Zulfikar Ghose.
p. cm.
ISBN 0–312–08545–1
1. Shakespeare, William, 1564–1616—Tragedies. 2. Death in literature. 3. Tragedy. I. Title.
PR2983.G47 1993
822.3'3—dc20 92–14227
CIP

They met me in the day of success; and I have learned by the perfect'st report they have more in them than mortal knowledge.

MACBETH: Act 1, Sc. 5

Contents

Author's Note

The chapter on *Hamlet* in this book is a revised version of my theory of the play first presented in an earlier book *Hamlet, Prufrock and Language* (London: Macmillan, 1978).

Z. G.

Prologue

The women all die first. Wearing 'fantastic garlands' of wild flowers, singing snatches of old hymns, Ophelia floats 'mermaid-like' in 'the weeping brook', and then sinks to her 'muddy death'. Hamlet's mother, the Queen, drinks the poison intended for him. Desdemona's breath is stopped by her husband Othello in the bed upon which she has had her maid lay her wedding sheets: the chaste bride is killed in her marriage bed. Of Lear's two 'pernicious' daughters, one poisons the other and the second has a knife pierce her heart. Lear's third daughter, the angel-like Cordelia, is hanged, and the old father, her corpse in his arms, fills the world with his howling. In the dead of night, fast asleep, Lady Macbeth walks with her eyes open, seeing nothing but her interior horror; her husband, who has 'supped full with horrors', hears a cry and is scarcely moved when he is told that she has died.

From the bodies of women flows life, and it is life that is stopped with their death. Ophelia is told by Hamlet, 'Get thee to a nunnery. Why wouldst thou be a breeder of sinners?'. Hamlet asks his mother not to go to her husband's bed. Othello kills his bride. Lear puts the curse of sterility upon his eldest daughter. Macbeth is the killer of children and himself has no heir. In *King Lear*, sex and breeding are for dogs and mongrel bitches. The world of Shakespeare's tragedies rejects life.

'World, world, O world!' laments Edgar from the nether world of his exile where the foul fiend leads him 'through fire and through flame', as if the living human being on earth were already in hell. Othello is given the illusion of arriving in heaven where he possesses a profound content, entering the heart of that radiance which is the soul's luminous habitat, but he must put out the light, and then put out the light.

Macbeth has found the self to be but a 'brief candle' and has become 'aweary of the sun'. Life and shadow are one.

Shakespeare's four great tragedies take the human soul into a bleak, dark interior where man is bound upon 'a wheel of fire', and in the final play we hear one cry:

> O horror, horror, horror! Tongue nor heart
> Cannot conceive nor name thee!

Hamlet: The Unweeded Garden

From the beginning of *Hamlet*, there is a cry for answers to mysteries. In the second line of the play, in the darkness of midnight, Francisco, hearing a voice call, 'Who's there?', shouts from his sentry-post:

> Nay, answer me. Stand and unfold yourself.

In the middle of the scene, Marcellus says:

> Good now, sit down, and tell me he that knows, . . .

There is an insistent demand for explanation: give us a meaning to these strange phenomena, tell us what these things purport: you are a scholar, Horatio, surely, you with all your knowledge can explain?

'That can I', says Horatio with the confidence of one who has no doubt that his learning has equipped him for answers to what is inexplicable to lesser minds. But presently he himself is exhorting the Ghost:

> If thou hast any sound or use of voice,
> Speak to me.

Speak to me. Use words. Construct a language so that I can know what I do not know and what I desperately desire to know. Even before Hamlet appears on the stage, before there can be any reference to the play's many themes and structural patterns (the revenge theme, madness, spying, the lost father, the mother's guilt, the diseased state, the Oedipus Complex, and so on), before we see any of the principal personages of the play, the sentinel Francisco who appears for no more than some three minutes and speaks only fifty-four words has established the theme of language and meaning. *Nay, answer me.* All the major characters will echo that phrase. Francisco also declares, almost casually, 'And I am sick at heart'. He does not tell us why, and we scarcely pay the phrase any attention, for there is no reason for so unimportant a character to be making so portentous a statement; but it is, we soon realise, also Hamlet's condition. *Stand and unfold yourself.* Hamlet could be asking that of language; or of life. From the very beginning of the play, ignorance is a torment. Who can say what is going on?

That can I. That is the scholar's glib assertion; his is the complacent pretension that learning can be applied to experience and all things satisfactorily explained. Horatio's answer to Marcellus is in a language of a young lawyer eager to appear knowledgeable:

Our last king,
Whose image even but now appeared to us,
Was as you know by Fortinbras of Norway,
Thereto pricked on by a most emulate pride,
Dared to the combat; in which our valiant Hamlet
(For so this side of our known world esteemed him)
Did slay this Fortinbras; who, by a sealed compact
Well ratified by law and heraldry,
Did forfeit, with his life, all those his lands
Which he stood seized of to the conqueror;
Against the which a moiety competent
Was gagèd by our king, which had returned
To the inheritance of Fortinbras
Had he been vanquisher, as, by the same comart
And carriage of the article designed,
His fell to Hamlet.

This one single sentence is followed by another which is thirteen lines in length, and the whole speech has the sort of clarity that may be read in the small print of a legal contract.

At the start of a play, it is hardly a language calculated to put the audience into the picture. And what's more, Horatio has just seen a ghost! Not something that happens every day that one, seeing an apparition, can coolly resume historical explanation in a language studded with legal jargon. Nor is it a language that Horatio's audience of Marcellus and Bernardo, who are two soldiers to whom he is presumed to be intellectually superior, can be expected to understand fully. It is a precise explanation, of course, but poor Marcellus, who had only asked *tell me he that knows*, must surely find it obscure or at least long-winded. But Horatio is not yet finished with his explanation, for, a scholar showing off his knowledge, he is unstoppable, and next launches a parallel between Denmark and Rome:

> In the most high and palmy state of Rome,
> A little ere the mightiest Julius fell, . . .

having demonstrated how well he can speak as a lawyer, Horatio is now showing off his possession of historical perspective and follows it a few lines later with an exhibitionistic display of poetical affectation:

> . . . and the moist star
> Upon whose influence Neptune's empire stands . . .

– using ten words for the simple word *moon* while he's talking, mind you, to a couple of soldiers! He might well have gone on and on had the Ghost not mercifully re-entered the stage. Thus, in two speeches, Shakespeare disposes of the scholar's language: it will not do, it is no answer to those simple but metaphysically profound words of Marcellus: *tell me he that knows*.

Horatio's self-assurance, his complete command over a technically complicated language as well as his mastery of rhetorical devices, all collapse on the reappearance of the Ghost. Here is a phenomenon he does not know and he can only appeal to it with the helpless words, 'Stay, illusion', for it cannot be fitted into the categories mastered by his learning. He can only address it with a hopeful formula: '*If* . . . etc.'

> If thou hast any sound or use of voice,
> Speak to me.
> If there be any good thing to be done
> That may to thee do ease and grace to me,
> Speak to me.

Two lines later, his voice calls a little more desperately:

> O, speak!

And appealing to the Ghost a fourth time, he cries

> Speak of it. Stay and speak.

It is the desperation of one who believes that all mysteries can be solved by rational explanation. Speak and you will be able to say who you are. Speak and I shall know. It is a scholar's illusion, of course; or a philosopher's; or a poet's: that language will reveal.

We have reached line 139 of the play and the second line, *Nay, answer me. Stand and unfold yourself,* is still echoing on the stage. As it will continue to echo throughout the play, and the word *speak* will be used again and again, right to the very last minute of the play when Fortinbras, calling for military honours for Hamlet's dead body, will ask for 'The soldiers' music and the rite of war' to

> Speak loudly for him.

The Ghost says nothing. And Horatio, frustrated seeker after truth who has given the impression of believing that speech equals explanation and rational discourse equals knowledge, says:

> . . . and by my advice
> Let us impart what we have seen tonight
> Unto young Hamlet, for upon my life
> This spirit, dumb to us, will speak to him.

Horatio does not say that the Ghost will speak to Hamlet because it looks like his late father. Marcellus had said when the Ghost first appeared:

> Thou art a scholar; speak to it, Horatio.

And Horatio, having failed to receive an answer, now thinks that Hamlet, presumably a greater scholar than himself, will be able to succeed. Hamlet might know how to probe this mystery which his, Horatio's, rhetorical outburst has failed to do: Hamlet might have a superior linguistic formula than the nervous cry *Speak to me*.

One learns few facts from the first scene. If there is any foreshadowing of action, it is only to do with young Fortinbras. Otherwise, we see the Ghost of the late king and hear some fancy talk from Horatio. There is little in the substance of the scene which ties up with the many interpretations which have been given the play.

But there is that word *speak* which appears again and again. Before any of the other themes are established, the scene clearly marks out the frontiers of that abstraction which is the ultimate business of literature: to test relationships between language and reality. If we could only hear or speak or arrive at the words which explained, we would *know*; and having the illusion that there is a necessary correspondence between language and reality, we are driven to despair when our words seem to reveal nothing. We are made mad by not knowing. We are left in the end with silence. As is Hamlet whose last word in the play is *silence*.

Hamlet, a play in two words:

> Speak.
> Silence.

There is one other idea buried in the first scene, in Horatio's speeches. When he gives his lengthy explanation concerning the war-like preparations he alludes to a dispute over territory, and in doing so he speaks the language of a lawyer; here is a world, parcelled out in plots of land, that is presumed to be certainly there, a land whose boundaries are fixed by legal definitions. Horatio is also given to affecting the language of poets and talks of 'the morn in russet mantle clad', a language which, being dependent upon metaphor, is sublimely the opposite of legal language with its hard insistence upon the established solidity of specification. We shall hear Hamlet scornfully mimic the language of lawyers in the graveyard scene; we shall also witness his fascination with the language of poetry. And we shall observe when we first see Hamlet and enter into his private thoughts that the plot of land in which he finds himself is 'an unweeded garden'. There is in Horatio's speeches a rhetorical rehearsal of two distinct languages each of which sets out to define reality; this is the central idea suggested by the play's first scene, and it relates directly to Hamlet's obsessive preoccupation with wanting to discover a language that offers an unambiguous revelation of reality.

*

Claudius, King of Denmark, complete master of the rhetoric of persuasion, certain of the effect his speech has on his court, speaking in a confident tone which asserts his authority and yet conveys his solicitous concern for the welfare of the state, disposes of his brother's death in fifteen and a half lines of an outrageous playing with shallow phrases which sound impressive to his sycophantic audience –

> Have we, as 'twere with a defeated joy,
> With an auspicious and a dropping eye,
> With mirth in funeral and with dirge in marriage, . . .

– and then has the audacity to add, probably in a lowered

voice affecting a tragic tone (which at the same time has a dismissive gesture to it, as if to indicate that life, after all, must go on), the hypocritical words: 'For all, our thanks'.

It is the consummate performance of a brilliant politician who must use words to maintain and strengthen his power; it is a most *calculated*, cunning use of language: it is pretending to a truth when the substance behind it is a lie. For Claudius, language is only a tool to be used skilfully and not a structure which imposes its subtle forms upon perceptions and renders reality a puzzle, which sometimes creates the illusion of knowledge and sometimes masquerades as knowledge itself. Claudius has no interest in conveying a meaning unless it serves his own ends, and he certainly has no interest in the idea of meaning itself; as a man of affairs, devoted to worldly ambitions, he can have no patience with epistemological enquiry. His first speech is a demonstration to his court that he is an effective ruler, the state's business is in efficient hands and he is to be trusted. A progressive new era is about to commence. To emphasise his understanding of events and his firm grasp of political reality, he disposes of Fortinbras in nine lines in which a reference to 'our most valiant brother' is a nicely calculated phrase which implies a protestation of innocence and also shows Claudius to be brilliantly opportunistic, and in which the earlier audacity of 'For all, our thanks' is matched by the superior attitude implied by the concluding phrase with which he puts Fortinbras in his place: 'So much for him'. And like a good, efficient ruler, he sends off his ambassadors to settle the matter with 'old Norway', giving them documents to convey to Fortinbras's uncle which contain precise and detailed language concerning the territorial dispute, with an insistence upon legal possession. Everything Claudius says is out to prove that he is very much in command: he is a man of his word and his word is to be translated immediately into action. And then, turning charmingly to Laertes:

> You cannot speak of reason to the Dane
> And lose your voice.

Claudius can listen to practical proposals: speak to him of the affairs of the world and he will respond with complete understanding: the word *speak* has no menace for him. Laertes, of course, is a political animal himself, a man of the same mould as Claudius (just as Horatio is of Hamlet's): Laertes had come to Denmark, he says, openly hypocritical, for the coronation (Horatio declares a little later that he came for the funeral).

Both Laertes and Claudius use language to advance themselves in the practical realm: meaning is important only in so far as it creates the right impression. When Laertes, all flattery and charm, bows before the King and begs his 'gracious leave and pardon', the King, who has no obligation to consult the young man's father, says with great charm and grace, 'Have you your father's leave? What says Polonius?' Both Claudius and Laertes must know that their speeches are making an impression upon the assembled courtiers who are hearing their words.

In contrast to them, Hamlet's first line, 'A little more than kin, and less than kind!', spoken as an aside (and therefore not intended to communicate an idea to anyone), is a play on words, an intellectual use of language intended more to gratify himself than to make an impression on his listeners; his last words in the drama, 'the rest is silence', are an abandonment of language which has not helped him. But here, in the first scene in which we see him, his concern seems more with appearance and reality and with the meaning and implications of a single word than with the immediate ordinary reality about which his mother questions him:

> Seems, madam? Nay, it is. I know not 'seems'.

He cannot talk without becoming involved in definitions, in the fine meanings of language. The Queen refers to 'thy noble father' and Claudius talks of 'these mourning duties to your father' but in his response Hamlet himself makes no reference to his father: his language is generalised:

'Tis not alone my inky cloak, good mother,
Nor customary suits of solemn black,
Nor windy suspiration of forced breath,
No, nor the fruitful river in the eye,
Nor the dejected haviour of the visage,
Together with all forms, moods, shapes of grief,
That can denote me truly. These indeed seem,
For they are actions that a man might play,
But I have that within which passeth show –
These but the trappings and suits of woe.

It is a pretentious little speech. Asked a simple question, he answers in the language of metaphysics, using such jargon words as 'forms' and 'denote', and indicates that the inner reality is something other than the outward appearance: it is not a statement which necessarily refers to his immediate situation. There is something within him which cannot be represented by appearance, something that is not a form or a shape, but the thing or the idea or the reality itself: it is the dream of the poet that form and meaning combine miraculously in a brilliant image of which the mind has an intuition but never that grasp which can be translated into words, or it is the delusion of the philosopher that beyond all forms there is some immaculate reality if only that language could be discovered which would reveal it: until that time of revelation, it remains buried within the consciousness of the sentient being, a continuously tormenting and oppressive presence.

Hamlet's speech is too abstract for Claudius, who launches upon a long statement of sweet reason, seizing the opportunity to demonstrate to the court a professedly genuine desire to be a loving step-father, and throwing in a couple of lines for the brooding philosopher:

For what we know must be and is as common
As any the most vulgar thing to sense,

but Hamlet does not even respond. Truth for him is not so easily reducible to an object of common sense in a language of such simplicity. No wonder his step-father and mother do not want him to return to Wittenberg: Hamlet is too much of a scholar already, what good will his obsession with precise speech, his compulsion to go beyond the mere illusion of meaning suggested by words and to comprehend reality itself, be if he ever is to play a role in the affairs of Denmark? Of course, the guilty King could want to have Hamlet where he could be kept under observation, but spies planted at the university could have kept the King equally well informed.

*

Left alone with his thoughts, Hamlet turns to the thought that torments him: there is no meaning to existence, better to become a drop of dew than carry the burden of sullied flesh.

> How weary, stale, flat, and unprofitable
> Seem to me all the uses of this world!

The *uses*: the practical events, the schemes and strategies by which one lives, the ordinary daily responsibilities. It's all worthless. Not because his father is dead and his mother has rushed into marrying his uncle; these are matters concerning ordinary reality which one must somehow endure: they touch one's feelings profoundly and produce a heartache, but they are not *problems* concerning existence; they engender emotional pain, but if they touch the intellect at all it is to make it more resolute in wanting to determine that the knowledge it possesses can be held to be irrefutably certain. There is no relation between Hamlet's thought and the mundane events in which his body is obliged to dwell. The opening lines of the first soliloquy comprise an abstract statement:

> O that this too too sullied flesh would melt,
> Thaw, and resolve itself into a dew,

and there is no connection between this abstraction, which is the intense focus of Hamlet's mind now that he is alone, and the action which has just taken place. Nor, when he goes on to wish that there were no religious law forbidding suicide, is there any suggestion that his longing to die is a response to his mother's behaviour; he says nothing about the mother as yet but proceeds to project a dismal picture of the world:

> . . .'tis an unweeded garden
> That grows to seed. Things rank and gross in nature
> Possess it merely.

It is this perception, which is given priority in his thoughts and is expressed so emphatically, which is the cause of Hamlet's intellectual and emotional desolation. The world as an unweeded garden is a potent image in his mind. His mind will continue to dwell on the metaphor until he arrives in the graveyard, the one scene in the play where (before the funeral party enters the scene) he is most at peace with himself, where his language is without that turbulence of expression which marks his speeches in so many earlier scenes, and where he can be said to be at home, having found the physical realisation of the symbol that has so obsessed his mind. The graveyard *is* the unweeded garden; in it may be found unsullied flesh that has melted and crawling there may be observed the things that are rank and gross.

Hamlet turns, in the first soliloquy, to ideas concerning his mother's behaviour as an afterthought. Life intrudes into his world of pure ideas and obliges him to concern himself with the events around him. Existence is meaningless but the petty business of carrying on living has unfortunately to be attended to. The philosopher does philosophy in the seclusion of his study but he's also got to carry the trash-can out for the garbage collectors who come on Monday morning.

Why did T. S. Eliot, in his essay on *Hamlet*, not see that here, in the very first expression of Hamlet's thought, was a formulation of the play's objective correlative? Eliot, one suspects, was looking at the play from a nineteenth-century perspective (for it is still hard to put *character* and psychological *motivation* out of one's mind) and attempting an interpretation by pondering the language which the play did *not* contain. The benefit to mankind has been that in the process of looking for what was missing in *Hamlet*, Eliot hit upon his theory of the 'objective correlative' but, ironically, saw no application of the principle he had discovered to the very thing, looking at which, gave him that principle; it is as if Newton, seeing an apple fall and arriving at the theory of gravity, were then to write an essay describing the remarkable phenomenon of falling apples possessing no gravity. Hamlet simply does not have the sort of emotion that an Othello is given to; his outbursts against Ophelia and his mother are not necessarily emotional. They could be, as we shall see, an expression of a *hatred of life*. The objective formula need not be a correlative of emotions only; it can be a correlative of pure ideas. In Act IV, scene iv, Hamlet is on his way to England and on 'a plain in Denmark' he encounters the Captain to whom Fortinbras has just given some instructions. Hamlet questions the Captain, asking if Fortinbras's army is going to invade the main part of Poland, and the Captain answers

> Truly to speak, and with no addition,
> We go to gain a little patch of ground
> That hath in it no profit but the name.

It is the first time we see Hamlet outside the Castle, and the first person he runs into is *speaking truly* to him and his language is a literal description of Hamlet's metaphor of the unweeded garden! Reality confirms the conclusions of abstract thought. The next time we see Hamlet it is in the grave-yard. There is no getting away from the *little patch of ground* which is the perfect object that represents the idea in his mind of the unweeded garden.

At the conclusion of his first soliloquy, Hamlet is so lost in thought that it takes him a moment to re-enter ordinary reality and recognise his friend Horatio who has come to tell him of his father's Ghost. 'And what make you from Wittenberg, Horatio?' he asks his university friend, and then repeats the question, 'But what, in faith, make you from Wittenberg?', as if he is astonished that anyone could want to leave a life devoted to thought and prefer to live in a royal court.

On hearing Horatio's account of the Ghost, and receiving to his own anxious question 'Did you not speak to it?' Horatio's answer that the Ghost had made a 'motion like as it would speak', Hamlet resolves to 'watch tonight' and if the Ghost appears again, he will 'speak to it . . .'.

It is his chance to discover the meaning of life as much as to find out if there has not been some foul play. To one who has been sitting in a mood of intellectual desolation, who finds worthless the uses of *this world*, and who, in spite of being a prince, thinks of the world as an unweeded garden, the possibility of speaking to the Ghost of his father has to be an opportunity to have the great metaphysical puzzle solved rather more definitively than any philosopher not lucky enough to receive such a visitor. There is the expectation that words will, finally, reveal. Let me not *burst* in ignorance, he will cry to the Ghost, give me knowledge, tell me . . . O speak!

*

LAERTES: Farewell, Ophelia, and remember well
What I have said to you.
OPHELIA: 'Tis in my memory locked,
And you yourself shall keep the key of it.
LAERTES: Farewell. (*Exit* LAERTES)

And in the very next moment when Polonius asks, 'What is't, Ophelia, he hath said to you?', she blurts it all out. For one who has *locked* a secret and given away the key to the now-departed brother, she does not hesitate for a second: thus, in the very first scene in which Ophelia speaks we notice the thoughtless way in which she contradicts her own words.

She uses language absent-mindedly, speaking phrases which are neat, sometimes poetically elegant structures, but there is not always a true understanding within her of what she has said. She merely goes through the motions of rationality. When she immediately gives away her secret, she does so not simply because she is an obedient daughter and Polonius an authoritarian father, for she could easily have lied – sisters do share secrets with their brothers about which they lie to their parents. No, Ophelia simply does not understand the words she uses, and if it can be said that our knowledge of the world is a measure of the language we understand and can articulate, then she has no grasp over reality; which is why it is logical that she should lose all hold over reality and go mad. (And in her madness sing: pure lyrics, those stunning combinations of words that reveal truth which is beyond apparent reality: for it is in her madness that she says, 'Pray let's have no words of this, but when they ask you what it means, say you this' – and then bursts into song which, it is therefore implied, is a form of communicating ideas not dependent merely upon the equivalence between a word and a thing but upon a factor which gives to ordinary language a dimension that in normal discourse is considered irrational. And Hamlet, following his feigned madness, will write a few lines to interpolate into the play within the play to see if the language of fiction, which is as much a lie as the language of madness as far as the so-called 'real' world is concerned, will not reveal a truth).

So, beginning with her speeches in the first scene in which she appears, Ophelia's language is seen to be irresponsible; she speaks words without knowing what she is saying; and the vagueness of her speech is indicative of the vagueness of her perception. Polonius is being literally precise when he admonishes her with, 'You do not understand yourself so clearly', and little does she herself realise the subtly self-reflexive irony of 'I do not know, my lord, what I should think'.

Polonius, offering to teach her, plays upon the word 'tenders' and is compelled to add parenthetically, ('not to crack the wind of the poor phrase . . .') – the compulsive aside of one obsessed by linguistic niceties; he is closest to Hamlet in his use of language, going so far as to comment upon the precise use of words ('That's good, "Mobled queen" is good.'), for he too wants to get to the bottom of things. But unlike Hamlet, his interest in language, while it has its academic and abstract moments, is utilitarian; for him, language is an instrument of discoveries to do with human behaviour. When Ophelia tells him of Hamlet's declaration of love, Polonius dismisses Hamlet's 'holy vows' as only words, they represent no meaning – and he knows the corruption that comes from the use of empty words.

> Do not believe his vows, for they are brokers,
> Not of that dye which their investments show,
> But mere implorators of unholy suits,
> Breathing like sanctified and pious bawds,
> The better to beguile. This is for all:
> I would not, in plain terms, from this time forth
> Have you so slander any moment leisure
> As to give words or talk with the Lord Hamlet.

He thus forbids her to *speak* and thereby reveal knowledge about herself. Expressing his ideas in an intellectually complex language, which mirrors his own level of perceiving reality, Polonius is shrewd enough to see his daughter is not so mentally developed; therefore, having already commanded 'Be something scanter of your maiden presence', he needs to repeat the command *in plain terms* to make sure Ophelia understands. And in forbidding Ophelia 'to give words or talk with the Lord Hamlet', Polonius perhaps fears that Hamlet with his superior mastery of language would not only ensnare Ophelia (for his holy vows are but 'springes to catch woodcocks') but also, and this would surely be worse, Hamlet might perceive Ophelia's essential stupidity and should the prince indeed be in love with her, possibly have second thoughts when he observes her dull mind. The protection of Ophelia's chastity is a good excuse to keep her away from the man who would be wonderful to have as her husband but who, given any sort of prolonged premarital intimacy, even an innocuous one, is bound to see the vapidity of her brain. 'I shall obey, my lord' is her dutiful answer; and the answer also of one who can respond only in trite phrases.

The situations in which Ophelia appears before she goes mad are too complex for her understanding; and the language she hears from her father and from Hamlet is invariably beyond her and each is obliged to say something in plain terms in order to get a response from her. In her meek conformity, she lives in a meaningless world until her madness relieves her of the responsibility to language and she can ignore the speech of everyone else and herself speak what gibberish comes to her mind: and in that total collapse of the relationship between language and reality, see visions.

*

Enter the Ghost again, and Hamlet cries out, 'Thou com'st in such a questionable shape / That I will speak to thee'. And then desperately,

> . . . O, answer me!
> Let me not burst in ignorance . . .

The violence inherent in 'burst' tells us something of his mental anguish. 'What may this mean', has the Ghost come 'With thoughts beyond the reaches of our souls?' All the pain of not knowing that has been growing within him explodes as he shouts:

> Say, why is this? wherefore? what should we do?

And when Hamlet decides to follow the Ghost, his first reason is not that the Ghost beckons him, but that it is silent:

> It will not speak. Then will I follow it.

The positioning of 'Then' is determined by more than the necessities of metre; and more than the sound of the line depends on where that 'Then' is positioned. The strong stress and the emphatically spoken word certainly draw attention to it, but the positioning also creates a definite cause and effect relationship between the two short sentences. It takes one right back to the opening of the play: *Nay, answer me. Stand and unfold yourself.*

> GHOST: Pity me not, but lend thy serious hearing
> To what I shall unfold.
>
> HAMLET: Speak. I am bound to hear.

But what the Ghost unfolds is not knowledge; he tells Hamlet nothing of the 'thoughts beyond the reaches of our souls', but gives only an account of how he, as Hamlet's father, had been killed by Claudius. The Ghost, who might have revealed the answers to all of Hamlet's metaphysical questions and made language redundant by providing the son with a vision into ultimate truth, can only talk at the petty level of his own former miserable vanity. (And incidentally, we have only the Ghost's word, and Hamlet's biased judgement, for the former King's merits. The Ghost says:

> O Hamlet, what a falling-off was there,
> From me, whose love was of that dignity
> That it went hand in hand even with the vow

I made to her in marriage, and to decline
Upon a wretch whose natural gifts were poor
To those of mine!

It sounds very much like the resentment of an elder brother at the younger brother being cleverer, for we have no evidence that the former King was in fact superior to Claudius. Certainly, after Claudius's performance in Act I, scene ii, it is difficult to imagine a shrewder head of state; whereas Hamlet's father seems to have been given over to luxury and indolence. And all he wants now, as a Ghost, is vengeance, that is, a placating of his own vanity.)

The Ghost has only an earthly story to tell, melodramatic and self-pitying at that, and he anticipates Hamlet's metaphysical curiosity by saying, 'But that I am forbid / To tell the secrets of my prison house . . .', so that Hamlet has no choice but to listen to words pertaining only to mundane events, words mainly to do with sullied flesh.

In a nice irony, some of the Ghost's imagery mocks Hamlet's desire to hear meaning. Having informed Hamlet that he cannot be expected to be told anything concerning the afterlife (though, tantalisingly, were the Ghost but free to speak, he could 'a tale unfold' that would make Hamlet's hair stand on end 'Like quills upon the fretful porpentine'), the Ghost prefaces his personal revelation with, 'Now, Hamlet, hear', which is precisely what the prince has been eager to do. The Ghost continues:

'Tis given out that, sleeping in my orchard,
A serpent stung me. So the whole ear of Denmark
Is by a forgèd process of my death
Rankly abused.

Here indeed is an unfolding and the receiving of meaning by the *whole ear*, but the message received is a lie which is meant to be accepted as truth. When the Ghost describes what really happened, he says how his brother stole upon him,

> And in the porches of my ears did pour
> The leperous distilment . . .

it is interesting to note that the poison was transmitted through the organ of hearing. Seeing the image of poison being poured into the ear, Hamlet must experience an unconscious terror, for language, too, when it is a distortion or a lie, can be a poison that is poured into the ear and instead of giving one a vision it only confirms one's death.

Horatio and Marcellus come in search of Hamlet after his encounter with the Ghost and when they ask him for an explanation, he can only offer them what Horatio bitterly calls 'wild and whirling words'. Poor Horatio: the Ghost, in the first scene, had not answered his *Speak to me* and now Hamlet, from whom he can reasonably expect an answer, will not speak either though his question is still, desperately, the same.

It is Hamlet's 'cursèd spite' to revenge his father's death. He would rather not be in this world which demands action, and it would have been easier for him if the Ghost had only given an intellectually interesting account of life after death. Instead, the Ghost has said nothing about death, and therefore revealed nothing about life, but merely talked about his own dying. In his emotional outburst at hearing the Ghost's story, Hamlet makes a solemn resolution:

> Yea, from the table of my memory
> I'll wipe away all trivial fond records,
> All saws of books, all forms, all pressures past
> That youth and observation copied there,
> And thy commandment all alone shall live
> Within the book and volume of my brain,
> Unmixed with baser matter. Yes, by heaven!

It is a formidable resolution for one so preoccupied with language and meaning. But it is only the heat of the moment. The next time we see Hamlet, in Act II, scene ii, he enters the stage, the stage-direction informs us, *reading on a book.*

*

Polonius's instructions to Reynaldo (Act II, scene i: a scene about which T. S. Eliot remarks 'for which there is little excuse') comprise an example of how language can be corrupted so that one can give the impression of telling the truth without actually doing so and, at the same time, without telling a lie. Language, we are to deduce, is not to be trusted; if we can utter propositions which have only the appearance of truth, and yet we ourselves know that they are not necessarily true, and which are not lies either, then what is language if not merely an *idea* in our minds, a structure which we accept or reject depending upon the beliefs we hold? We cannot rely upon the words we use to contain the truth we like to believe they do because we ourselves can put the same words to corrupt usage: therefore, how can we expect *language* to tell us anything about reality?

Reynaldo is to find 'By this encompassment and drift of question' and not by honest enquiry; he is to be ambiguous, subtle, suggestive; he is to put words into the mouths of the Danes in Paris in order to discover what Laertes is up to: Reynaldo is to carry out an elaborate deception but by using words which have only the semblance of truth. Reynaldo is to 'put on him / What forgeries you please'. Polonius sums it up neatly: 'By indirections find directions out.'

If Laertes is indeed the scoundrel that the 'forgeries' will portray him to be, then they will not be 'forgeries' at all but accurate descriptions which everyone will recognise to be true; and the implication is that should Laertes actually be an upright man and a dutiful son keeping to his father's precepts, then Reynaldo can always say that he was thinking of someone else, it has been a case of mistaken identity: *in either event*, language would appear to have been used to utter truth: and that in itself is the underlying lie behind Polonius's scheme which he spells out to Reynaldo by giving him examples of sentences he should use:

> 'And in part him, but,' you may say, 'not well,
> But if't be he I mean, he's very wild
> Addicted so and so.'

It is, he says, a 'bait of falsehood' with which to catch the 'carp of truth'.

Polonius is both a statesman and a scholar. He is sharper than Claudius in his understanding of language as a tool to serve a political end; he also understands language as a thing in itself (having been, like Hamlet, interested in drama when he was at the university), and in this respect he is intellectually superior to Hamlet whose word-games are almost a mockery of himself and who is trapped by language, finding an endless necessity to use words and never being able to know the world behind those words, being obliged merely to carry on experiments in grammar, while for Polonius language is never without a practical use. If the two men had literary careers, Hamlet would be a poet, Polonius a critic.

Eliot did not see the relevance of the Reynaldo scene because he was looking at the play's action and the psychological motivation of its characters and, surprisingly for so great a poet, not looking at the language. In his essay, Eliot is dismissive of Horatio's famous

> But look, the morn in russet mantle clad
> Walks o'er the dew of yon high eastward hill,

because it reminds Eliot of the relatively immature Shakespeare of *Romeo and Juliet* but, as noted before, Horatio in the same scene (I, i.) also uses the language of a keen young lawyer, and if we observe that one of the central preoccupations of the play is to use examples of speech to indicate the quality of the speaker's mind and his understanding of reality, then surely Horatio's 'russet mantle clad' is perfectly acceptable as showing that Horatio, a scholar, is overimpressed by certain types of expression and loses no opportunity to use them, especially among people who are intellectually his inferiors. It is an affectation common to young people who have recently come down from a university. We are the victims of the language we have learned, especially when we believe that that particular language has liberated our minds and given us the freedom to observe the world as it really is, which, of course, is a nice illusion since we do not observe that the language of our emancipation itself consists of chains of words with the only difference that they are of another complexity than we had comprehended before. Far from being a scene for which there is little excuse, the Polonius–Reynaldo scene is a neatly objectified dramatisation which correlates very precisely with the play's larger theme of language. As do the speeches concerning the Players and Hamlet's instructions on how to speak a speech.

*

In the same scene is Ophelia's description of Hamlet coming to her in an incredibly distracted manner. She says to her father:

> My lord, as I was sewing in my closet,
> Lord Hamlet, with his doublet all unbraced,
> No hat upon his head, his stocking fouled,
> Ungartered, and down-gyvèd to his ankle,
> Pale as his shirt, his knees knocking each other,
> And with a look so piteous in purport
> As if he had been loosèd out of hell
> To speak of horrors – he comes before me.

It is bizarre behaviour, to say the least, and it could be that this has been one of Hamlet's first attempts to show himself as being mad. But I doubt it. In fact, I doubt Ophelia's words. The image of Hamlet, 'his knees knocking each other' and the rest of Ophelia's description, is too fanciful to be believed, for there is little else in the play to suggest that

Hamlet attempts to advertise his madness in any other way than through a manipulation of language; the only reference to a physical manifestation of the madness is the King's remark in II, ii that Hamlet's 'exterior' does not resemble 'that it was', but that hardly suggests the extraordinary image as described by Ophelia – an image more of a wild, than a mad, man. If Hamlet seriously loves Ophelia (as he later declares in the graveyard scene that he did), he is not going to come before her in the guise of a demented fool, which he does not before others when he appears to have gone mad. And if his interest is only to seduce her, then his technique is going to be subtler than simply dropping his stockings to his ankles. No. Instead of an image of Hamlet's feigned madness, what we have here is a foreshadowing of Ophelia's own real madness. Her mind is inventing an unreality, and she is scared. It should be noted that she prefaces her description by saying to her father:

> O my lord, my lord, I have been so affrighted!

The irony is that Polonius does not see the symptoms of madness in his daughter but instead, translating her words according to his own beliefs, immediately concludes that Hamlet has been driven to distraction by love for his daughter. It is a perfect example of how when someone does *speak* to us, we hear something else. We are interpreters and translators of what we hear and understand only that which accords with our beliefs. There is no reason to doubt anyone whose speech does not violate the rules of grammar and it is only when it does that we begin to think that the person must be mad.

*

Polonius comes to the King and Queen and informs them that he has discovered why Hamlet has gone mad. The King responds excitedly: 'O speak of that! That do I long to hear'.

The King, too, is tormented by an anxiety to know, though, unlike Hamlet's, his is only a mundane anxiety prompted not by a desire for revelatory knowledge but by a wish for personal security. Presently, Polonius begins to speak and his words seem so like the prolegomenon to a philosophical tract that the simple-minded Queen stops him and implores, 'More matter, with less art'. Polonius answers:

> Madam, I swear I use no art at all.
> That he's mad, 'tis true: 'tis true 'tis pity,
> And pity 'tis 'tis true – a foolish figure.
> But farewell it, for I will use no art.

Speak clearly, tell us what you really mean: that is the simple-minded person's cry while the scholarly mind, trying hard to say precisely what it means, becomes involved in labyrinthine phrases and protests that it is only saying what in fact is the case; and such a mind is also so obsessive an analyst of the structure of its own language that it often compulsively comments (in an aside) upon the form of words it is in the process of uttering.

Polonius is not so much a long-winded fool, which he is sometimes represented to be, as a mind which is torn between wanting to use a complex language in order to communicate precisely the complexity of his ideas while being aware, at the same time, that to most other minds such seemingly convoluted formulae seem bizarre, and so will have a self-critical aside ('a foolish figure') or add a reassuring phrase at the end of a complicated sentence ('I will be brief.'). He comments compulsively not only upon his own but also upon others' language, as has been observed with his remark upon the 'mobled' queen, and when he reads Hamlet's letter to Ophelia he cannot resist remarking on one of Hamlet's phrases: 'That's an ill phrase, a vile phrase; "beautified" is a vile phrase'.

Who cares? Certainly not Claudius and the Queen, who are only interested in the *matter* of Hamlet's letter, which he is showing them as proof of the source of Hamlet's madness, and not in its *art*. It is this sort of aside which has made many actors interpret Polonius as a lovable old imbecile, provoking an easy mirth among audiences, thereby missing the point that what Shakespeare is doing is to focus attention upon the way in which language is used. There is nothing of the old fool in Polonius when he says

> If circumstances lead me, I will find
> Where truth is hid, though it were hid indeed
> Within the centre.

Unlike Hamlet, however, his interest in language is not allied to a quest for knowledge, for Polonius seems to have concluded already that we can know nothing:

> My liege and madam, to expostulate
> What majesty should be, what duty is,
> Why day is day, night night, and time is time,
> Were nothing but to waste night, day, and time.

It is futile, he implies, to speculate about things and abstractions. But aware that language offers a scope for speculation, Polonius turns that upon language itself, deriving pleasure from a fine phrase. While he enjoys an academic pleasure in playing language games, he never neglects the practical business of life and therefore his speeches are more calculated to achieve immediate ends than to purchase some refined intellectual gratification. When he has read Hamlet's letter to Ophelia, he makes a long speech to the King on the subject of his loyalty:

> . . . what might you,
> Or my dear majesty your queen here, think,
> If I had played the desk or the table book,
> Or given my heart a winking, mute and dumb,
> Or looked upon this love with idle sight?

He wants the King and Queen to know that instead of encouraging Ophelia to receive Hamlet he has expressly forbidden her to do so; he is anxious that they know that he thinks, and has said so to Ophelia, that Hamlet is far above Ophelia's rank for her to entertain any notion of accepting his love. In suggesting this, Polonius proclaims that modesty which he no doubt hopes will be over-ruled; all his protestation that Hamlet is of too high a rank for Ophelia is calculated to make the King and Queen disregard the question of social degree: he has observed Hamlet's interest in his daughter and, seizing the first item of evidence, he has begun to manipulate a favourable outcome by pretending to be eager to prevent precisely that which he wishes to happen.

*

And now: '*Enter* HAMLET *reading on a book*'.

> QUEEN: But look where sadly the poor wretch comes reading.

The poor wretch has gone mad, apparently, but the audience knows it is only a feigned madness. It is difficult for the modern audience not to be aware of some three hundred-odd years of criticism which has tried to account for this madness. Even Eliot talks about it: 'For Shakespeare it is less than madness and more than feigned. The levity of Hamlet, his repetition of phrase, his puns, are not part of a deliberate plan of dissimulation, but a form of emotional relief.' Eliot is again looking at psychology and not at language (and, incidentally, Eliot's own language sounds more impressive than the meaning it conveys: that first sentence seems to have been prompted by a desire to utter paradox. Sometimes, a neatness of phraseology convinces us that we have said something remarkable).

But we do have a mad person in the play, Ophelia, and

her madness is represented as a failure of language to be rational: words used with no seeming logic. Of course, at the literal level of the play's action, whether we see it as merely a revenge tragedy or as containing one or more of the many other themes, such as spying, the reasons for Hamlet's feigned madness are obvious enough: he does not want to seem to appear responsible, he wants the freedom to observe for as a madman he can be in places where his presence would otherwise be suspicious to the King, and so on. But if we pursue the theme of language, then the feigned madness is explicable in an entirely different way.

One thing which distinguishes mad people from the sane is that they have no hold over language. Rational speech is an attempt to communicate and to understand meaning and there is a tacit assumption between the sender and the receiver of a message that they both speak 'the same language'. Words tell us not only what a thing is but also what is behind it, how it is to be interpreted. Also, language is our tool of epistemological enquiry, we attempt to comprehend the objects of experience through words. But no philosopher has ever been able to come up with a final theory of knowledge because each has ended by constructing only a new combination of words. In the end, there are only words; and a grammar to govern the usage of those words, a grammar which human beings themselves have invented in the first place. We live in a chaos of sentences, kept sane by grammar's illusion of order. We are condemned to muttering endless sequences of words and have yet to discover a single sequence that can penetrate the barrier of language. Our excursions into the sciences (involving us in the invention of complex mathematical languages, computer models of the universe, and technologically new modes of perception, such as the Hubble telescope,) show us other barriers rather than reveal knowledge.

Once the realisation strikes one's mind that no language-proposition is ever going to represent a true perception of reality, then one is confronted by the ultimate failure of the human intellect. What can we do? Let us experiment, let us reverse our normal procedure. Instead of expecting words to be rational, neatly continuing the attractive formula of cause and effect, let us see what happens when the words are exaggeratedly irrational and blatantly nonsensical. As in the drama of Jarry and Ionesco. Sanity has not given us the truth we seek, let us attempt insanity. As in Pirandello's *Henry IV*. Rational language has not helped us, it stubbornly refuses to tell us anything about life and even the dead father, returning as a ghost, cannot enlighten the son who is obliged to resume reading his books. So, let us, as scientists do, submit our propositions to a deliberate contradiction, apply the test of the negative, examine anti-meaning (just as some modern poets have written anti-poems in order to write meaningful poems which they have believed no longer possible by using the linguistic procedures of traditional forms) and see if a deliberate confusion will not create a new order in one's mind.

Speak and *silence*. And in between a feigned madness, an experiment in speech calculated to do the opposite of *unfolding* oneself to see if anti-language will not do what language consistently fails to do.

A revealing comparison can be made with some twentieth-century literature – Beckett's plays and novels, for example. Listen again to Lucky's speech in *Waiting for Godot*, that violently rapid and maddened flow of words at the heart of the play, to see how the writer needs to tear at language in the desperate rage for meaning. Or observe how the language of *Waiting for Godot*, an early play, becomes a silence in *Breath*, a late play, or how the compulsive rationality in *Murphy* and *Watt*, the first two novels, gives way in *How It Is* and *Lessness*, two later fictions, to an attempt to deny grammar its traditional role; the seemingly irrational language of the later works is a sort of feigned madness, and these texts, when one begins to make connections, seem truer in their comprehension of reality than the earlier, seemingly rational works. The collected works of Samuel Beckett can be said to take place within the mind of Hamlet, Prince of Denmark. Beckett is not the only writer to have attempted the technique of apparent logical irresponsibility. T. S. Eliot did so. Indeed, apparent literal incoherence has been so common in twentieth-century literature that we accept it as a valid technique and are more inclined to raise our eyebrows at simple, direct expression.

Hamlet's madness, projected primarily through language, while it serves the action at a literal level, is also an experiment in language. And the play *Hamlet*, it seems to me, is the objective correlative of literature.

*

Hamlet's encounter with Polonius has been all word-play and one need only quote in passing Polonius's question, 'What do you read, my lord?', and Hamlet's answer, 'Words, words, words', which a twentieth-century philosopher will surely agree is a much more precise answer than if Hamlet had said, 'Beowulf'.

More word-games follow with Rosencrantz and Guildenstern. Indeed, Act II, scene ii, the longest in the play, has examples of the various types of language used in *Hamlet*: from the King's statesmanlike words of dissimulation and the Queen's insipid simple-person's speech to the exchange of wit between Hamlet and Rosencrantz and Guildenstern, including the seeming distortions of language induced by the feigned madness; going on to the language of fiction when Hamlet recalls a speech from a play; and ending with a soliloquy in which Hamlet at last seems to confront his problem but finds a reason to defer its solution a little longer.

Hamlet's excitement at seeing the Players is cerebral; it is not merely a love of the theatre, nor is it due to the realisation that he can use the Players to test the guilt or innocence of the King: his excitement at first is that of one who is fascinated by a stylised literary language. 'I heard thee speak me a speech once, but it was never acted. . . .' How delicious to hear a language that creates its own indubitable truth which, having been 'never acted', has remained locked in itself and which has not suffered the violence of being subjected to the test of vulgar experience!

There is a genuine spontaneity to Hamlet's excitement: 'You are welcome, masters, welcome, all. I am glad to see thee well. Welcome, good friends.' And without waiting for the formality of the Players responding to his greeting, though he has addressed several of them individually, he says, 'We'll have a speech straight. Come, give us a taste of your quality. Come, a passionate speech.'

He cannot wait to hear words which create complete structures of meaning without reference to personal experience. A poem, a sonnet by Shakespeare, say, or a soliloquy in a play called *Hamlet*, for example, can be just such a structure constructed on formal principles of aesthetics or of rhetoric, bounded, that is, by the rules of its own grammar and yet not confined within any space, being timeless and immortal, unlike the human body, and therefore seeming to possess an access to truth which remains inevitably elusive in common experience. Artistic formulations have a potential for perfection not available to ordinary existence where we must suffer from colds and constipation; but since in literature the formulations are made up of the very same words with which we conduct the business of ordinary existence, we are therefore driven to believe that language ought to allow us visions to do with our own lives which in literature it does to the abstract concept of Life. And is not the inability to distinguish between these two languages sometimes a source of madness – hallucinations, schizophrenia, delusions of the self? A mad Ophelia is as much a visionary as Blake, singing songs the language of which has transcended common experience.

The speech Hamlet wants to hear is from a play which was too good to be a popular success; it was, he says, 'an excellent play, well digested in the scenes, set down with as much modesty as cunning. I remember one said there were no sallets in the lines to make the matter savoury, nor no matter in the phrase that might indict the author of affectation, but called it an honest method, as wholesome as sweet, and by very much more handsome than fine.'

Here is Hamlet with all manner of private problems, who has recently seen his father's Ghost and who has been pretending to be mad, going on and on about the art of drama. But it is not merely that Shakespeare is giving his contemporaries a lesson in the 'honest method' of his own art (and that is not an uncommon practice among writers: see, for example, *Jealousy* by Alain Robbe-Grillet in which two characters discuss a novel by contrast with which, it is implied, the novel in Robbe-Grillet's reader's hands is the one with the 'honest method'). And it is not merely that Hamlet's mind has quickly seized the idea that here is a chance to put reality to the test of fiction. It is also the expression of a craving to experience again, as he no doubt did as a student, that ecstasy produced in the mind when language, inventing a reality on which to impose its symbols with tensions appropriate to art with no necessary reference to life, transcends the known facts of that experience and captures an idea which evokes a luminous comprehension without the mind being able to so say what it is that it has understood, although it is certain that it has understood much more than the words it has heard.

The fascination with fiction common to all human beings is as enduring as the fascination of men and women with their own selves: whether we are drawn to fiction because, at the simple level, we can be comforted by the conviction that someone else's representation of people and situations and places coincides with our own view of reality; or,at a slightly higher level, where the fiction goes a little beyond its subject-matter and conveys a few ideas, because we are seeking an expression of those explanations which we have already formed, but only vaguely; or, at that level where literary language has created a fiction which we call art, because we want more than simply to relate to another being's world, more than to be given an interesting and a seemingly plausible explanation: we want, seek, and discover in art that elusive sensation given the miserable word *vision*.

If Hamlet really only wanted the play to prove his uncle's guilt, then all he needed was something at the popular level, a play the action of which would be understood by all. But either the court at Elsinore has been so cowed by Claudius that it dare not see what it is made to witness or it does not have the capacity to interpret fiction in terms of reality: for the truth is that the only person to understand the play (apart from Horatio who, however, has been coached in advance by Hamlet) has been Claudius, and language has once again failed to convey the meaning expected of it; or, Hamlet, driven to excess by his own desire to hear the language of art and have the play serve the double function of proving the King's guilt and providing an ecstasy to Hamlet's own imagination, has put on a play at his own level, that of a poet, but his audience has consisted of people familiar only with the lesser levels of art. Had everyone else seen the truth, Hamlet would have needed only to appeal to the court and won his case and got rid of Claudius without the need of personally having to murder him. He has uttered a language through the play but his audience has only heard words and that, too, without seeing a relation between the words and reality. Hamlet has seen more than the King's guilt, he has seen the failure of language. Here is language and there is the world: but if there is a connection between the two, it is only in the mind of the creator of those words, and the reality one has believed one has represented might well be, in the minds of one's listeners, a description of some alien planet's geography. One never knows what other people understand.

The speech which Hamlet wants the Player to recite begins, as Hamlet himself remembers (and proceeds compulsively to declaim its first thirteen lines):

> 'The rugged Pyrrhus, he whose sable arms,
> Black as his purpose, did the night resemble

> When he lay couchèd in the ominous horse,
> Hath now this dread and black complexion smeared
> With heraldry more dismal. . . .

Here is a refined literary language, entirely artificial in its assembling of phrases to insinuate a dominant image into the mind of the audience: *sable, black, night, ominous, dread, black,* and *dismal* are a constellation of words belonging to the idea of darkness. It is a self-sufficient world which resembles reality in having objects and at the same time a context of abstraction. The sense of inevitability, or the impression in the audience's mind of truth, comes not from the relationship of these words with the reality that we know but from a conviction engendered by the vocabulary, the grammar and the general figure of speech holding the words together in one's imagination: here, the guarantee of truth is contained in the words themselves, in their apparently accurate relationship with each other. We do not need to know anything outside the passage itself to believe what we are being told, for the language which suggests its ideas as *conclusions* does so by first making us believe that it is clearly declaring, within the entire verbal formula, the *premises* on which those conclusions are founded. The entire thing is nothing but an impression in our minds; it could be a sequence of propositions of Euclidean geometry where our impression of understanding would be influenced by our acceptance of certain axioms.

Literary language can be, and often is, a self-contained structure: once the poet has committed himself to some such statement as 'Shall I compare thee to a summer's day?' the rest of the sonnet is obliged to investigate ideas of time and mortality just as Euclid, once he has committed himself to the principle of the straight line, cannot create a geometry dependent upon wavy lines that snake about the universe; furthermore, the commitment to the sonnet form, rather than, say, to a sestina, is going to prompt a balanced neatness of expression, with a rounded, logical ending, which form of expression, if it pleasingly fulfils the appropriate aesthetic principles, will also heighten the sense of truth suggested by the completed imagistic pattern. While at the literal level the Players offer Hamlet a chance to test his own hypothesis of the King's guilt, he is nevertheless thrilled, so to speak, by the structure of straight lines which grow out of each other to form an interesting pattern because in that pattern the truth is undeniable, possessing an internal logic quite independent of what might happen in one's own daily existence.

And when the Players have gone, Hamlet is overwhelmed:

> Is it not monstrous that this player here,
> But in a fiction, in a dream of passion,
> Could force his soul so to his own conceit
> That from her working all his visage wanned,
> Tears in his eyes, distraction in his aspect,
> A broken voice, and his whole function suiting
> With forms to his own conceit? And all for nothing,
> For Hecuba!

Seeing how a fictitious passion can elicit tears, for a moment Hamlet is led to entertain the belief common to human vanity that if a writer would only make one's own real passion his subject-matter then his fiction would 'drown the stage with tears', but by the end of the soliloquy Hamlet settles for what effect mere art might have 'to catch the conscience of the king'. He appreciates the strength of language as metaphor; the subject-matter of one's own life, however strong, can never match the force of literary invention: to approach a truth concerning human existence, the best medium is that special language which is not concerned with existing humans, but which, drawing its imagery from life, assembles those universals which are descriptive of the human race. As does the play *Hamlet*.

*

KING: And can you by no drift of conference
Get from him why he puts on this confusion,
Grating so harshly all his days of quiet
With turbulent and dangerous lunacy?

Can you not, by speaking to him, get him to unfold himself? The function of the spies (Reynaldo, and Rosencrantz and Guildenstern) is to establish another approach in order to discover what someone really is and the method of the spies is prescribed as an artful and deceptive use of language: Reynaldo must put 'forgeries' upon Laertes, and Rosencrantz and Guildenstern must employ a 'drift of conference'. The prescription comes from Polonius and from Claudius, the two shrewdest manipulators of language in the court.

We never hear what came of Reynaldo's mission, but it is interesting to observe that Hamlet matches Claudius's spying upon him by himself arranging the play at which he and Horatio will spy on Claudius; and he will match what Claudius has called a 'drift of conference' with an even more elaborately deceptive employment of language – the seemingly irrelevant speeches of the play. And just as Claudius has hoped that Hamlet will tell the truth about himself to Rosencrantz and Guildenstern, so Hamlet believes that 'murder, though it have no tongue, will speak' when confronted by a literary representation of its own guilt.

Claudius finds 'much content' on hearing that Hamlet is disposed to being entertained by the Players. Both to him and to the Queen, the play represents the idea of mere *play*, or pastime, something to take one's mind away from one's own problems: the language of fiction will have a diverting effect and might well be the tonic to relieve the oppression suffered by a melancholy mind; while to Hamlet the play is to serve another function, that of carrying on an experiment with language to see if a fictive representation of reality might not precisely be the verbal formula of an undeniable truth.

Two languages come together in the idea of the play: that

of make-believe, as observed by that part of the audience seeking diversion, and that which is the source of belief, as observed by Hamlet; and since these two languages are actually one language, the common words which everyone hears, this one language is therefore a metaphor which is susceptible to varied interpretation: to some it is purely an invention which can have no meaning unless the words refer to an already known world; to others, those with the sensibility of a Hamlet, no world can be known unless the language is first posited, and to these it is reality which must always remain an invention made possible by the rigidly logical structure of language: a reality made accessible and then believable by one making up a fiction, one who has never suggested he was doing anything other than telling a story, a lie.

*

Polonius and the King are to spy upon the contrived meeting between Hamlet and Ophelia. She is instructed to 'Read on this book' – Polonius thus hitting upon the correct strategy to draw Hamlet. Claudius, suddenly touched in his conscience by Polonius's reference to 'devotion's visage', is led to draw a graphic image in a confessional aside:

> The harlot's cheek, beautied with plast'ring art,
> Is not more ugly to the thing that helps it
> Than is my deed to my most painted word.

One remarks upon the sequence here of *art, the thing, deed,* and *painted word*. There at the centre one has

thing/deed

flanked by

art *word*

especially that word which is *painted* and therefore, nearly a synonym for *art*. Here is a nice reversal: just as Hamlet hopes that the play with its art (or, that language which blatantly is not true) will reveal a truth, so Claudius wants his language to be so full of art that no one will observe that it is masking a lie.

Claudius is, in a sense, Hamlet's anti-self, his nature being pragmatic where Hamlet is given to abstraction; villain though he is, Claudius is always interesting while Hamlet, for all his virtue, is sometimes an utter bore; Claudius is a manipulator of the world around him, he is an artist among politicians, while Hamlet is rarely more than a naive metaphysician or a mediocre poet.

And now to his most famous soliloquy, which contemplates a deed but really is only a meditation on an idea. It is straining credibility if we take the soliloquy literally. Clearly, Hamlet does not have the egocentricity of one who is potentially a suicide: he dwells not so much on himself as on the world, the problems which concern his own life certainly torment him but do not absorb him entirely for the problem of existence is a greater torment. Surely, he is not so cut off from life as to have no pressing anxieties, and one need not draw up a list – his father's death, his mother's behaviour, his love for Ophelia, the threat to his own life – to appreciate the point that a good many facts of his life are of a bewildering complexity; but their nature is not that which induces people to commit suicide and Hamlet has no reason associated with his immediate reality to be contemplating suicide. His formulation, 'To be, or not to be', is the phrasing of an idea which needs to be tested; it is the logical continuation of the idea which began with the 'unweeded garden'; all that is happening is that his mind is continuing to debate the imponderables: only, the debate has become heightened by the poignancy of what is going on in his own life although as far as his *existence* is concerned not even the Ghost's appearance has changed anything.

It is doubtful if the sharp-witted Prince of Denmark ever

suffered from 'the proud man's contumely' (being 'very proud' himself, as he presently says to Ophelia, and being highly gifted in the utterance of contumely, as when he attacks his mother); it is doubtful, too, if he had any legal suit pending or ever had to put up with 'the insolence of office' or if he truly felt that his 'patient merit' was not rewarded; and surely the Prince would be the last person in Denmark 'To grunt and sweat under a weary life'. Perhaps the 'oppressor's wrong' and the 'pangs of despised love' can be said to refer to his own experience, but much of his speech is impersonal and generalised, composed of propositions with which to pursue an intellectual enquiry. Such language as 'the whips and scorns of time', 'Th' oppressor's wrong' and 'the law's delay' belongs to an essay an English earl might write for the *New Statesman* but is hardly the phraseology of a suicide note. A person does not commit suicide because there are six or seven generalisations about the oppressed human condition on his mind.

Hamlet is not contemplating suicide but testing the meaning of life by positing its very opposite, and in his conclusions he is very much like a Beckett character who knowing that life is meaningless realises that death will not solve anything, for it will not guarantee the elusive meaning but either prolong the anguish in the after-life ('the dread of something after death . . . puzzles the will') or, if there is no after-life, make the one life even more absurdly meaningless. And like many of Beckett's characters, Hamlet is obliged to pass the time by talking to himself, now testing one hypothesis and now another. The 'pale cast of thought' makes action futile, especially the action which is the extremest of all – self-murder. And yet the mind must compulsively go on combining words, the ceaseless flow of language cannot be checked in whatever time or place the body dwells, and besides there is always the possibility that the next new combination of words might be the formula of revelation.

The encounter with Ophelia follows. Hamlet, who has been weighing propositions in his mind, his abstract introspection happening in a generalised language, suddenly tears into Ophelia with some of his most devastatingly scholarly language, so that he has hardly begun when the poor girl, sensing the confusion in her own mind, cries out:

What means your lordship?

She has already made her little token speech, a pretty little poetic gesture that a refined young lady might learn the formula of at a finishing school:

> My honoured lord, you know right well you did,
> And with them words of so sweet breath composed
> As made the things more rich. Their perfume lost,
> Take these again, for to the noble mind
> Rich gifts wax poor when givers prove unkind.

That ought to have been enough to make the man she believes is in love with her to enfold her in his arms, but Hamlet does not even appear to listen to her and a moment later he launches his tirade.

> Ay, truly; for the power of beauty will sooner transform honesty from what it is to a bawd than the force of honesty can translate beauty into his likeness. This was sometime a paradox, but now the time gives it proof.

She is dumbfounded, and he adds: 'I did love you once.' At last a sentence she can understand and respond to: 'Indeed, my lord, you made me believe so'. But Hamlet goes on:

> You should not have believed me, for virtue cannot so inoculate our old stock but we shall relish of it.

Again she is speechless and Hamlet adds a simpler statement: 'I loved you not', completing a neat paradox. 'I was the more deceived', she wails self-pityingly.

Hamlet's speeches to her become violent and are rapidly spoken (the preponderance of monosyllables – 'be thou as chaste as ice, as pure as snow' – demands a fast, agitated speech from the actor); they contain ambiguous ideas which are probably beyond Ophelia's comprehension. She can answer only when he adds a simple statement when the main torrent of his ideas has passed – for example, 'Where's your father?'

Ophelia can speak at her own pace again only when he has abandoned her:

> O what a noble mind is here o'erthrown!
> The courtier's, soldier's, scholar's eye, tongue, sword,
> Th' expectancy and rose of the fair state,
> The glass of fashion and the mould of form,
> Th' observed of all observers, quite, quite down!

Typically, like all simple people whose understanding of language is at the level of mundane reality and who can rarely see beyond the narrow world of their own self (Ophelia: 'And I, of ladies most deject and wretched'), her response to Hamlet's complexity of language is to believe that he must be mad.

Hamlet has attacked Ophelia for the sexuality, or the principle of procreation, which her womanhood represents. His violent speeches to her are not an attempt to prove his madness to anyone who might be overhearing him. He has been thinking of life and death: *To be, or not to be. . .* : death, he has concluded, offers no resolution to the problem of existence. And here is the fair Ophelia, the woman, the womb of life. And to her he says: 'it were better my mother had not borne me'. The woman before him, the fair Ophelia whom he loves, contains within her the potential for creating life and, what is worse, his own desire for her makes him an accomplice in breeding life. In his present mood, he, who believes that his own conception was an appalling act, turns away with revulsion ('No, not I . . .') on hearing Ophelia say

> My lord, I have remembrances of yours
> That I have longèd long to redeliver.

For in the sexual act, too, he would give her that which she would redeliver. What follows in this scene is not madness but a rage against life.

Only the King, perceiving that Hamlet's language 'was not like madness', comes closest to understanding the abstract nature of Hamlet's torment:

> Love? his affections do not that way tend,
> Nor what he spake, though it lacked form a little,
> Was not like madness. There's something in his soul
> O'er which his melancholy sits on brood . . .

Being burdened by his own guilt, however, Claudius is obliged to translate his own ignorance of what it is in Hamlet's soul into a potential threat. He had better not take any chances. Hamlet must away to England. It is a perfectly wise move, for this kind of Hamlet is a threat not only to the King but also to the state: the poet must be banished, the dissident put away; and the appearance of doing the right thing for the security of the state will camouflage his own need to eliminate Hamlet.

But Polonius, despairing at losing the Prince as a potential son-in-law, comes up with a stratagem – let the Queen meet Hamlet in private and ask him to tell the truth, with Polonius himself listening from a concealed position.

Everyone is anxious to hear the meaning which each is convinced is surely there: Polonius that Hamlet loves Ophelia, the King that Hamlet suspects him of killing his brother, and Hamlet is looking at the idea of meaning itself. While there is dramatic conflict in the play at the level of human action, there is this more complex conflict at the level of human thought.

*

HAMLET: Speak the speech, I pray you, as I pronounced it to you, trippingly, on the tongue.

This is one occasion when Hamlet can tell another to speak in such a way that he, Hamlet, can hear precisely what he wants to hear down to the subtlest gestures and the most distant of nuances. If only the exhortation to *speak* made by everyone from Francisco to Claudius could elicit a similarly rehearsed response! All problems of the relationship between language and reality would vanish then, for we, commanding the speech we wish to hear, would then be the creators of reality.

Hamlet's instructions to the Players are not merely Shakespeare's attempt to lay down some basic principles of acting but they contain an experiment of Hamlet's to see if unreality cannot be made to assume the characteristics of reality to such a degree that it has the very appearance of reality so that he can observe if this reality, made to the special order of a human will and bounded so neatly by time and place that it can be comprehended fully, cannot offer that vision which ordinary existence has so far failed to give him. Hamlet can be dismissive of ordinary people, 'the groundlings, who for the most part are capable of nothing but inexplicable dumb shows and noise'. He has the intellectual's, and the artist's, contempt for ordinary people who are content with surfaces; but 'inexplicable dumb shows' are also to be despised because they are inexplicable and *dumb*, which is to say they do not serve the command *Stand and unfold yourself*, for they do not *speak*.

Hamlet's main stricture, of course, is that the actors should be natural: 'Suit the action to the word, the word to the action, with this special observance, that you o'erstep not the modesty of nature'. The play he wants to see has to be so lifelike that it is reality itself. His intention to devise a play in which he can catch the conscience of the King has already exceeded itself and become an enterprise calculated to test reality itself. But when performed, the play provides him with nothing other than circumstantial proof of the King's guilt, though seeing art achieve that effect briefly produces in Hamlet a crazed excitement.

(The dialogue between the Player King and the Player Queen, which jingles along in dully rhyming couplets of the *prove/love* and *strife/wife* variety, is so boring that, were it not for his confessional soliloquy in the following scene, one would think Claudius had walked out like some modern critic at a new play, impatient with trite dialogue. One does wonder, though, why Claudius who has been so cunning in manipulating the court simply did not sit it out, pretending that he was having a great time. But, of course, there's so much a writer can do to make his characters consistent. And incidentally, I have never seen a production of *Hamlet* which has contained the entire play within the play; most producers have used only the dumb show – which makes a nice comment on modern audiences, reducing us all to groundlings!)

Hamlet is so exhilarated by the apparent success of the aborted play in proving the King's guilt that he breaks out into verses (much as Ophelia does later when she goes mad) and calls for music. Art has succeeded, at least partially, in having shown Hamlet what he wanted to see, and he seems to go quite mad with excitement. But first Rosencrantz and Guildenstern return demanding that he put his 'discourse into some frame, and start not so wildly' but make 'a wholesome answer', and then Polonius comes back to say solemnly and without his usual convoluted phraseology that 'the Queen would speak' with him. Yet once more, the instructions which come from the world outside the self are that one find a proper form for one's language and that one use words which are understandable. Rosencrantz says quite simply: 'She desires to speak with you in her closet ere you go to bed'.

There is little reason for the scene to be prolonged another sixty or so lines but Hamlet, having just experienced the ecstasy of what artistic language can achieve, is being drawn back to the ordinary use of words, which activity all his earlier experience has taught him leads nowhere; and so, when Guildenstern makes a hypocritical statement about his love for him, Hamlet instinctively takes a recorder from the Players and says, 'I do not well understand that'. And then, immediately, holding up the recorder, Hamlet asks, 'Will you play upon this pipe?'

This pipe, this instrument: within which are contained all combinations of musical phrases. But Guildenstern can do nothing with it, no more than a foreigner with a language he does not know but who is given a dictionary of it and asked to make combinations of words in such a way that they add to a poem. It is in utter frustration that Guildenstern replies, 'But these cannot I command to any utt'rance of harmony. I have not the skill'.

Hamlet can then abuse him and Rosencrantz – 'there is much music, excellent voice, in this little organ, yet cannot you make it speak' – for their presumption that they can play on him, make him *speak*. It is significant that the example he has chosen with which to make his point is to do with creating meaningful sound out of an object which in itself is inert and silent, like the human tongue. The entire thrust of the scene is to counter-point the original 'Nay, answer me' with 'yet cannot you make it speak'. There follows the little exchange with Polonius concerning the cloud.

HAMLET: Do you see yonder cloud that's almost in shape of a camel?
POLONIUS: By th' mass and 'tis, like a camel indeed.
HAMLET: Methinks it is like a weasel.
POLONIUS: It is backed like a weasel.
HAMLET: Or like a whale.
POLONIUS: Very like a whale.

Polonius is remarkably submissive and disinclined to argue in this exchange, but he is the only person in the play who is likely to understand that Hamlet's point is not merely to assert himself but that what Hamlet is suggesting is something that he, Polonius, cannot deny: it is to do with the arbitrariness of words, for here 'camel', 'weasel' and 'whale' are words which do not refer to the class of things we define as camels, weasels and whales, but are *merely* words that signify nothing but appearances or only their sounds. Also, the three sounds could be like the sounds made on a recorder by one who does not know how to play it but, idly picking up the pipe, blows upon it, without harmony. *Peep, peep, peep*; or perhaps *peep, poop, pip*; or perhaps, if the instrument is the human tongue, *camel, weasel, whale*.

It could also be, of course, an attempt to demonstrate his continuing madness and Polonius's quiet acquiescence could be the delicate manner of one not wanting to aggravate another's disturbed mental state; but the imagery, and the form in which Hamlet puts it, does indicate that even when he is most profoundly engaged in attending to the problems of guilt and retribution his mind cannot avoid testing correspondences between words and the reality they represent. To have acquired certainty of Claudius's guilt is a minor victory; the real prize would be to have certainty of knowledge.

Having received Polonius's acquiescence that so formless a thing as a cloud can contain the idea of things which we think we know (thus reaching an epistemological dead-end, for the words do not necessarily refer to objects but are only themselves and therefore without meaning), Hamlet can then, satisfied that his enquiry into language can give him nothing, return to his mundane reality and attend to his mother. But what will he do on seeing her?

> I will speak daggers to her, but use none.
> My tongue and soul in this be hypocrites:
> How in my words somever she be shent,
> To give them seals never, my soul, consent!

Speak; words. He can never escape from language.

*

The King, who had been the first to perceive that 'what he spake . . . / Was not like madness', now says of Hamlet

> I like him not, nor stands it safe with us
> To let his madness range.

The play just abandoned, his own guilt nearly made public, Claudius desperately needs everyone to believe what he himself knows to be false. These are the first words we hear from him since he walked out of the play and one observes how he has summoned all his resources of statecraft, one of which is his cunning manipulation of language of which this opening sentence is a superb example. In this sentence, in which the greatest stress falls on the syllable *mad*, the speech implies a presumption that Hamlet's madness is an established fact and is calculated to foster in others the idea that the madness not only explains what has happened – that the play was the work of a madman – but also that it is dangerous to the state to let such a madman remain free.

Left alone, the King broods upon his guilt, wondering how a formula of language could serve as sufficient prayer.

> But, O, what form of prayer
> Can serve my turn? 'Forgive me my foul murder'?

Only in heaven 'the action lies / In his true nature' but in 'the corrupted currents of this world' we may continue to deceive; for here, we are attached to things ('My crown, mine own ambition, and my queen') and our language cannot separate us from these things. Prayer cannot help Claudius, not only because his repentance is insincere as long as he keeps 'those effects' for which he committed the murder but also because of the idea that if the language of things can be used to deceive then what certainty is there that the language of heaven is always true?

> My words fly up, my thoughts remain below.
> Words without thoughts never to heaven go.

Words are forever detaching themselves from ideas, and human thoughts can never become the pure forms of heaven no matter what intensity of transcendental effort we exercise.

While the King is at prayer, Hamlet, on his way to his mother, sees him, realises he has a chance to revenge his father, but says, 'That would be scanned', meaning that he should look into his proposition, and proceeds to make an investigation of logic in order to understand the word 'revenge':

> A villain kills my father, and for that
> I, his sole son, do this same villain send
> To heaven.
> Why, this is hire and salary, not revenge.

It sounds like a student's first exercise in syllogism. It is not revenge because it does not guarantee the uncle will go to hell; also, the reality does not conform to the propositions in his mind and Hamlet gets carried away inventing the reality he would prefer – which invention, characteristically, is a literary structure:

> When he is drunk asleep, or in his rage,
> Or in th' incestuous pleasure of his bed,
> At game a-swearing, or about some act
> That has no relish of salvation in't –
> Then trip him, that his heels may kick at heaven,
> And that his soul may be as damned and black
> As hell, where to it goes.

The language of his imagination is richer than the logic with which he has just tried to analyse the immediate situation; certainly, the poetic image in his mind of Claudius kicking his heels at heaven is more interesting to him than what he would see if he now stabbed Claudius in the back – in which case all he would see would be a dead body. In the alternative which he projects, he is not responsible to facts but, like a poet, takes delight in the invention of imagery to pursue a private vision, thus relieving himself from the obligation to participate in his immediate reality. It is not procrastination; the immediate reality is not exciting enough for him to perform what has to be an extraordinary deed – he is quite capable of action but, as with the pirates on the high seas and as in the duel with Laertes, Hamlet needs a poetic or a dramatic setting: if there has to be action, it must be carried out under the illusion of significance or for that extreme reason, survival.

*

Polonius, coming to inform the Queen that Hamlet is on his way, says, just before he withdraws to eavesdrop, 'I'll silence me even here'. It is a perfect statement for one who has spoken so many words and, of course, there is a poignant irony to what he has said, for he is minutes from being silent for ever. In the previous scene, he had informed the King of his plan to eavesdrop on Hamlet's encounter with his mother and his last words to the King were

> I'll call upon you ere you go to bed
> And tell you what I know.

He had made a promise to bring him knowledge that, it is anticipated, will be a revelation of truth. He will call, ghost-like almost. Now, coming to the Queen's chamber where that knowledge is to be gained, he does indeed receive knowledge, but it cannot be communicated, for it is knowledge of his own death.

While Polonius positions himself where he will soon be overwhelmed by silence, the dialogue begins between mother and son:

> QUEEN: Come, come, you answer with an idle tongue.
> HAMLET: Go, go, you question with a wicked tongue.

The dialogue is at once about the *kind of language* one may use; the Queen has been instructed to 'be round with him' and Hamlet is determined to 'speak daggers to her'. It is immediately apparent even to her that in any dialogue he is going to outwit her, for she simply does not have the resources of language to be able to talk to him, so that within ten lines she nearly abandons the attempt, saying, 'Nay, then I'll set those to you that can speak', clearly implying that she herself cannot. Hamlet has been deliberately asked to go to her so that she may get him to unfold himself, but if she cannot speak the words necessary to achieve that result, then someone else will, someone who *can speak*.

The vehement note in Hamlet's response makes her panic, and a moment later Polonius is killed, Hamlet no doubt hoping that it is Claudius who is hiding behind the curtain, for that would fulfil his recent fantasy of killing Claudius when he is doing something demonstrably immoral. It is interesting to note in passing that his victim is unseen – it is an *abstract* murder, almost as if Hamlet were killing an idea for which rational words had failed him. The action of killing a human being seems to have no effect upon him at all, he might as well have swatted a fly; his mind is entirely upon what he has to *speak* to his mother, and if his emotions are overwrought, it is because he has to use a language so violent that when he does so, she cries out:

> What have I done that thou dar'st wag thy tongue
> In noise so rude against me?

His answer is an aggressively eloquent flow of speech, the words unfolding her self to the Queen so that she pleads

> O Hamlet, speak no more.
> Thou turn'st mine eyes into my very soul . . .

But Hamlet will not stop now that words appear to be revealing truth, and the Queen cries desperately

O, speak to me no more.
These words like daggers enter in mine ears.
No more, sweet Hamlet.

Still he hurls the words at her and still she cries, 'No more.' And then: 'Enter GHOST'. She is saved. The words which were holding a mirror up to her, making her begin to see 'black and grainèd spots' in her soul, can now be rejected as having no meaning, for it is with great relief that she says, seeing Hamlet talking to the Ghost, 'Alas, he's mad'. The Ghost's appearance has the effect of terminating Hamlet's verbal violence and making him adopt a softer tone when, following the Ghost's last words, 'Speak to her, Hamlet', he changes his language from being abusive to one which shows a solicitous concern, so that the Queen is more inclined to be understanding.

Hamlet may well suffer from the Oedipus Complex and his statement to his mother – 'go not to my uncle's bed' – could be quoted to support that thesis. But as was observed in the scene with Ophelia, Hamlet has a horror of procreation – 'it were better my mother had not borne me': now he pleads with his mother to refrain from sex; not necessarily because of some buried guilt, some suppressed fantasy in which he has slept with his mother or desired her sexually, but possibly because the event of the mother being penetrated is a *repetition* of the very event that led to his own conception. In the mind of one who finds worthless all the uses of this world, to whom the world is an unweeded garden and existence without meaning, that one event is charged with so much disgust that it has assumed the texture of evil.

*

KING: There's matter in these sighs. These profound heaves
You must translate; 'tis fit we understand them.

From *Nay, answer me* (Act I, scene i) to *You must translate* (Act IV, scene i) the vocabulary has changed but the speaker is making much the same demand.

The language we hear, or the signs we observe, need to be translated and what we believe to be meaning, or truth, is often no more than a conviction that we have understood, which is to say that the speech we have heard is translated, or interpreted, in the mind according to a formula already embedded there. But while the French word *l'eau* might become *water* in the mind of an Englishman who knows French, or *low* in the mind of one who does not, a shimmering on the horizon can also become *water* in the mind of one crossing a desert: the idea into which a word is translated depends on factors quite independent of, and sometimes entirely irrelevant to, that word. When we use language, our presumption is that our correspondent has eaten the same excellent dinner that we have and that he is not likely to mistake our description of snow for the icing on a cake. And, of course, frequently we are obliged to confess to incomprehension and to say: *You must translate.*

When the Queen does translate, she does so in a manner calculated to convince Claudius of his own preconception, for the first word she uses in her explanation is 'Mad'. She has learned to speak in Claudius's own cunning manner.

> Mad as the sea and wind when both contend

she says of Hamlet, choosing a figure of speech which can accommodate the word 'mad' without her actually needing to say that Hamlet is mad, for the 'mad', in her context, can mean 'enraged'. It is her most subtle speech in the play; she who has wanted 'more matter, with less art' is here herself artful, wanting to disguise from Claudius the true nature of her meeting with Hamlet; and she succeeds in creating a misleading impression without having told a lie. Reynaldo could not have done better.

Claudius instructs Rosencrantz and Guildenstern to find Hamlet and tells them to 'speak fair' to him while he himself, with the Queen, will 'call up our wisest friends / And let them know . . .'. Meanings are to be divulged, but there is no guarantee that after hearing them anyone will *know*.

Hamlet no longer needs to feign madness but appears madder than ever, mocking Rosencrantz and Guildenstern with insults (and it is Rosencrantz who now does the real feigning, saying, 'I understand you not, my lord' when there is little not to understand and surely he has enough experience of figures of speech to comprehend the trite image 'sponge') and running away from them when they are about to take him to the King.

It is now important to the King, and therefore to those serving him, to continue to believe that Hamlet is mad. Claudius says, 'How dangerous is it that this man goes loose!' not because Hamlet is a lunatic murderer at large who might strike another innocent victim but because Hamlet has revealed that he knows Claudius's guilty secret: and that line of Claudius's is yet another example of how his language is invariably charged with cunning, being always calculated to establish as truth that appearance which serves his own political or personal end. Indeed, he is not only an interpreter of appearances who broadcasts convenient distortions of the truth but is also sometimes their creator, engineering reality for popular consumption:

> To bear all smooth and even,
> This sudden sending him away must seem
> Deliberate pause.

While to Hamlet the uses of this world are worthless because they do not show him *the world*, Claudius is of that world of which he himself manipulates the uses.

When Hamlet is brought to Claudius in Act IV, scene iii, there seems to be genuine bewilderment in the King's 'What dost thou mean by this?' Perhaps he is only provoking Hamlet to utter some complicated speech which will be observed by the witnesses present to be a lunatic's ravings, but for a moment he does appear confused, and the question, 'What dost thou mean by this?' is profounder than at first appears, demanding rational explanation while wanting evidence of irrationality and at the same time being expressed in a tone that echoes the anguish of someone for whom every question involving meaning has the potential for transcendental revelation. When Hamlet's answer is in the simple 'Nothing but . . .' formula, Claudius immediately reverts to his earlier firmer tone, that of an interrogator demanding a confession, and asks, 'Where is Polonius?' And with ruthless efficiency, he resolves the business in hand to his own advantage. His words are heard by the courtiers present as solicitous expressions of good-will towards Hamlet while their real purpose is to seize a self-serving opportunity; Hamlet is to go to England, the witnesses hear, for his own 'especial safety' while the King's secret instructions will be for his execution.

*

Act IV, scene iv: *A Plain in Denmark*. And this is where Hamlet, enquiring of Fortinbras's Captain the nature of the army's engagement, is informed

> Truly to speak, and with no addition,
> We go to gain a little patch of ground
> That hath in it no profit but the name.
> To pay five ducats, five, I would not farm it,
> Nor will it yield to Norway or the Pole
> A ranker rate, should it be sold in fee.

Truly to speak. Here is one, an anonymous soldier, telling Hamlet the truth. All the warlike preparations, all this martial show; and all for a worthless *little patch of ground*. The actions of both the Poles, in defending it, and the Norwegians, in invading it, are meaningless and yet both parties are prepared to die for it; here is a representation of humanity which does not pause to consider the absolute futility of its actions but goes about asserting the belief that what it does is *right*, thus substituting the fact of an unbearable existence with a stimulating morality: when reality fails us, an abstract language gives us a reason to be. It is the delicate hypocrisy of religions which knowing that we can never see offer us visions; and it is our subtle delusion that since we cannot see, therefore there must be visions available to us. Our vanity will not put up with a little patch of ground.

Hamlet's soliloquy which follows shows him at first to be chastising himself for having delayed the revenge. But the *occasions* which *inform against* him are the visible facts of the world and his despair is that he cannot escape the trivial banality of existence, for after the opening statement, his first *thought* is one more philosophical proposition:

What is a man,
If his chief good and market of his time
Be but to sleep and feed? A beast, no more.

But this, he reasons, is unacceptable:

Sure he that made us with such large discourse,
Looking before and after, gave us not
That capability and godlike reason
To fust in us unused.

Discourse, that understanding through language, and a capacity to observe cause and effect, ought to produce more tenable convictions than man has been able to arrive at; instead, he is either a beast who has no concept of responsibility or a rational creature of such complexity that he is absorbed entirely in 'Looking before and after', searching always for that primal 'before' and that ultimate 'after' discovering which could guarantee meaning.

– I do not know
Why yet I live to say, 'This thing's to do,'

Sith I have cause, and will, and strength, and means
To do't.

He is not deluding himself about his will–the statement is a factual one; his failure comes from his desire to discover from the rational processes within his own mind that statement which would be an absolutely irrefutable instruction that he perform the action. Notice, too, the irony of 'I do not know', an irony sustained by the isolated position of the phrase in the structure of the verse where it seems to be suspended almost outside the context.

Unlike Hamlet, Fortinbras 'Makes mouths at the invisible event' and does not need 'great argument' to send twenty thousand men to their death for no commendable reason. Fortinbras is not only a reminder to Hamlet of what kind of prince he himself ought to be but also an example of a leader who invents causes, one who uses language not to ask questions but to give orders, who substitutes a metaphysical quest with physical conquest, who, throughout the play, seems to be marching about the frontiers of Denmark with his feet firmly on the ground, finally to be seen as the only one capable of inheriting the earth – which final fact is one of the loveliest subtleties of the play: it is Fortinbras who goes to capture the little patch of ground and if the patch is the play's symbol for the earth, then Fortinbras, with an irony which he will never comprehend, fully deserves to succeed to the throne of Denmark and, in his own terms, inherit the earth for which Hamlet no longer has any use.

Hamlet concludes the soliloquy with the resolution

O, from this time forth,
My thoughts be bloody, or be nothing worth!

Let language-propositions be replaced by action-propositions: this is the same momentary resolution to act that Hamlet had expressed in Act I after seeing the Ghost where, too, he had resolved to dismiss intellectual preoccupations from his mind; but in this speech that final phrase is curious: 'be nothing worth' means more than just 'worthless'. If we see 'nothing worth' as an inversion (which it is, for the sake of the rhyme), the phrase can mean 'worthy of nothing'. If one could utter a proposition which showed the true worth of *nothing*, a word of enormous consequence to ideas concerning being, we could make a great leap in this matter of language and knowledge. The unobtainable vision desperately sought for resides not in the world of objects that we perceive as reality but in a world of *nothingness*; otherwise it could not constitute *vision*.

*

Ophelia has gone mad and the Queen says: 'I will not speak with her'.

One cannot speak with the mad, they talk a different language; one does not wish to hear them either, they might utter something so mad that it is a revelation of truth. And the Queen has already been battered by words: she had to beg Hamlet to *speak no more*, for she had believed him to be mad and his enraged language had suddenly revealed him as both sane and in possession of truths she had not wanted to confront, and here is Ophelia who is decidedly mad and God knows what she might not say. No. *I will not speak with her*. The Queen is terrified of words.

GENTLEMAN: She is importunate, indeed distract.

As was Hamlet in Act I when he saw his father's Ghost and called to him importunately, 'O, answer me! / Let me not burst in ignorance . . .'. The Gentleman then says of Ophelia that she

. . . says she hears
There's tricks i' th' world . . .

that she 'speaks things in doubt' and that

> Her speech is nothing,
> Yet the unshapèd use of it doth move
> The hearers to collection; they aim at it,
> And botch the words up fit to their own thoughts,

and while it is certain that there is nothing in her words there is nevertheless much there, 'unhappily'. A language that conveys nothing is still conveying the idea that language can be used to express no meaning. And sometimes a meaningless language (as, for example, of literary criticism) is heard as conveying significance because we 'botch the words up', interpret them, according to an established intellectual prejudice. There is no understanding that does not make a cross reference to belief.

Ophelia's madness is *heard* in her speeches and her songs; it pours into the ears of her hearers as had the poison into the ear of the King asleep in the garden. She whose language had no responsible relationship with reality but went about giving an impression of logical speech has now abandoned the world of appearances. Something in her mind tells her that there are tricks in the world, and these are not only deceptions which she has experienced, finding herself cheated of the happiness she had expected, but also deceptions to do with her understanding of the world itself: she has arrived at Hamlet's perception but not having Hamlet's rational language can make nothing of it: *Her speech is nothing*, her words are 'nothing worth'. And when Laertes sees her later in the scene, he says, 'This nothing's more than matter'. It is matter itself, this *Nothing*.

And when she enters, she utters a simple truth in her madness: she sings, and the imagery of her songs is to do with death and procreation. The mad are seen to have reverted to some prelapsarian innocence; our pity for them is mingled with an awe and sometimes, as with a John Clare, we consider them sentimentally as divinely blessed. Ophelia sings with a poet's simple beauty:

> He is dead and gone, lady,
> He is dead and gone;
> At his head a grass-green turf,
> At his heels a stone.

Or she can be bawdy:

> Then up he rose and donned his clo'es
> And dupped the chamber door,
> Let in the maid, that out a maid
> Never departed more.

But all the visionary truth that her madness can reveal is to do with breeding and dying. The quest for meaning has been eliminated: there is no 'before and after' for the mad.

She breaks off her song to say, 'Lord, we know what we are, but know not what we may be'. And 'Pray let's have no words of this'. She is the only one who can say with perfect conviction that *we know what we are,* but the language with which she reveals this is of 'unshaped use': her hearers can understand her only intuitively but are convinced that there is nothing to understand. *Pray let's have no words of this,* let us listen to the song. The philosopher ends with silence, the poet dies singing.

*

HORATIO: What are they that would speak with me?
SERVANT: Seafaring men, sir. They say they have letters for you.

It is as if another Ghost were appearing to Horatio, for there is a suggestion about 'seafaring men' as messengers from another world, an idea hinted at by what Horatio goes on to say:

> I do not know from what part of the world
> I should be greeted, if not from Lord Hamlet.

And when the sailors give him Hamlet's letter, Horatio reads in it, 'I have words to speak in thine ear will make thee dumb'. We are reminded of what the Ghost had said to Hamlet, that he 'could a tale unfold' that would make Hamlet's 'hair to stand on end'. Now Hamlet, metaphorically visiting Horatio from another world, too has a tale to unfold; and like the Ghost, his tale will concern his own body.

Hamlet's return as if he were a Ghost is also suggested by the phrase 'my sudden and more strange return' in the letter he writes to the King, whose first comment on reading it is, 'What should this mean?', and to whom Hamlet's return must indeed be ghostlike since he had every expectation that he would be dead by now.

What should this mean? is doubly significant, being on the literal level a perfectly natural question for the King to ask; and secondly, in terms of the play's preoccupation with language and knowledge and the attempt to arrive at that combination of words which creates a meaning which, hitting upon a correspondence between language and reality, at last breaks down the barrier between the two, the question echoes the central obsession of the play. If we could only say what *this* meant!

Much of this scene (Act IV, scene vii), however, consists of the dialogue between Claudius and Laertes in which there first is another brilliant example of the use of language to persuade, in which Claudius uses not mere suggestion, as he did in Act I, scene ii, but sound political reasoning; and second, after the letter from Hamlet has been received, the subtle use made of it by Claudius to let Laertes believe that it is his own idea to become a fellow-conspirator and to be the instrument of Hamlet's death –'. . . if you could devise it so / That I might be the organ'. Once Claudius has manœuvred Laertes to this commitment, he makes certain of Laertes's loyalty by flattering him, and it is pertinent to note that the device he uses parallels the kind of instructions which Polonius had given Reynaldo (the lesson of 'put on him / What forgeries you please', and Claudius, indeed, uses the word 'forgery' in his speech). In order to flatter Laertes, Claudius praises a Norman visitor; using precisely the kind of language which Polonius was at pains to instruct Reynaldo to use, he says of the Frenchman:

> I have seen myself, and served against, the French,
> And they can well on horseback, but this gallant
> Had witchcraft in't. He grew unto his seat,
> And to such wondrous doing brought his horse
> As had he been incorpsed and demi-natured
> With the brave beast. So far he topped my thought
> That I, in forgery of shapes and tricks,
> Come short of what he did.

The speech is long for what it says but the calculation behind it is to create a sense of wonder, and identification, in the mind of Laertes, and no sooner has Laertes recognised the man than Claudius says:

> He made confession of you,
> And gave you such a masterly report
> For art and exercise in your defence,
> And for your rapier most especial,
> That he cried out 'twould be a sight indeed
> If one could match you.

The flattery continues for half a dozen more lines, becoming more exaggerated. The technique is transparent, and if one wonders why it is drawn out at such length one answer has to be that Shakespeare is presenting a comprehensive example of the language of corruption which he had, through Polonius, earlier defined in structural outline. So carefully studied is Claudius's technique that watching Laertes accept his flattery as truth, he leaves him in a delicate suspense for a moment, saying, 'Now, out of this – ', while pretending that he is thinking to himself, so that Laertes, who by now is totally committed to the King's cause, asks anxiously, 'What out of this, my lord?' And with greater subtlety, Claudius, instead of answering, asks Laertes a question, and so involves him in an abstract language in a lengthy speech of philosophical and theological overtones to do with parental love that when he finally asks

> Hamlet comes back; what would you undertake
> To show yourself your father's son in deed
> More than in words?

Laertes is obliged quickly to make that answer which will most convince Claudius of his willingness to act and which Claudius has, indeed, put him in a corner to utter: 'To cut his throat i' th' church!'. It is a statement which even in its violent extremity has logically got to be the culminating conclusion of all that Claudius has said.

It is a victory of the King's political shrewdness to have converted an inflamed rebel not merely into an ally but also into a passionately committed conspirator and his only weapon has been a cunning language. The victory is almost ruined by the Queen coming to announce that Ophelia has drowned herself and when the King says to her at the end of the scene, 'How much I had to do to calm his rage!', he is expressing both his fear that Laertes might again take to rebellion and also a statement about his artful employment of language with which he has attempted to win over Laertes.

*

Now to the Churchyard and '*Enter two* CLOWNS', a scene which begins apparently as comic relief but the humour of the clowns consists of their misuse of language: to themselves there is nothing funny in what they are saying.

> It must be *se offendendo*; it cannot be else. For here lies the point: if I drown myself wittingly, it argues an act, and an act hath three branches – it is to act, to do, and to perform. Argal, she drowned herself wittingly.

If we substitute the malapropisms with *se defendendo* and *ergo*, the Clown could be a young student at Wittenberg showing off his recently acquired mastery over rhetoric. One has seen people, even educated ones, use language with similar imprecision while they suggested an aura of perfect conviction that they were being precise: nothing sustains the illusion of truth than simple human conceit, a belief in personal infallibility. Only other people are clowns.

The dialogue of the clowns in *Hamlet* is a parody of serious discourse, for their language has the surface appearance of formal correctness but yet is seen by the audience to be laughably absurd. It is an absurdity that reflects back upon language itself, showing the seemingly logical speech to be ridiculously illogical. And like both Hamlet and Ophelia who break into verses and songs, the former in the ecstasy of believing he has observed the truth about the King's guilt and the latter in the ecstasy of madness, the Clown, too, breaks into song the substance of which is sexuality and old age, not unlike that of the verses sung by Ophelia. Truth is again discovered to be the banality of procreation and death but the Clown suffers from no anguish while uttering this truth, spending his life digging grave after grave and having to stand in each grave that he digs without being bothered by the symbolic nature of his action.

Hamlet, who has symbolically been sitting on the edge of a grave throughout the play from the moment we see him reflecting upon the unweeded garden, who has seen his father come back from the grave, and who in his 'To be or not to be' soliloquy has pondered life beyond the grave, now enters the stage to stand physically beside one and says of the skull thrown out by the Clown, 'That skull had a tongue in it, and could sing once'.

Not speak but *sing*, which in the hierarchy of sounds is a superior activity, for speech is condemned to observe responsibility to meaning while song is a self-contained poetical structure of which the idea can be comprehended intuitively. But that song is lost now and the skull reveals nothing: 'Here's fine revolution, an we had the trick to see't'.

The Clown throws out another skull and Hamlet says: 'Why may not that be the skull of a lawyer? Where be his quiddities now, his quillities, his cases, his tenures, and his tricks? . . .' It is a long speech that follows, concerning the inevitable fate of lawyers and great land owners. Why does Hamlet feel compelled to go on and on? The point about the greatest politician or lawyer being reduced to skull and bones is obvious enough to the most naïve imagination. It is all those *words* – 'quiddities', 'quillities', and so on – which are exciting Hamlet's brain; the special language of legal contracts which are designed to eliminate, or minimise, the errors of interpretation and to establish certainty of possession is to do with material things, with little patches of ground: the vocabulary of this language is calculated to make definitions precise and to eliminate doubt: what *is* is believed to *be*. The irony which bemuses Hamlet ('They are sheep and calves which seek out assurance in that' he says) is that even so specially structured a language which tries to leave no room for doubt is finally of no help to the people who utter it, and Language is once again seen as merely appearing to be relevant to the human condition.

There follows Hamlet's exchange with the Clown when he asks, 'Whose grave's this, sirrah?' and the Clown answers, 'Mine, sir'. Again, the humour comes from a play on words.

HAMLET: I think it be thine indeed, for thou liest in't.

CLOWN: You lie out on't, sir, and therefore 'tis not yours. For my part, I do not lie in't, yet it is mine.

And then:

HAMLET: What man dost thou dig it for?
CLOWN: For no man, sir.
HAMLET: What woman then?
CLOWN: For none neither.
HAMLET: Who is to be buried in't?
CLOWN: One that was a woman, sir; but, rest her soul, she's dead.
HAMLET: How absolute the knave is! We must speak by the card, or equivocation will undo us.

Although the Clown is seen to be a simpleton, one to whom things must be spelt out to avoid confusion, and therefore a source of humour, he is in fact correct in his speech and that answer, 'One that was a woman, sir; but, rest her soul, she's dead', is as precise as was Hamlet's 'Words, words, words' in answer to Polonius's questions about what he was reading.

HAMLET: How came he mad?
CLOWN: Very strangely, they say.
HAMLET: How strangely?
CLOWN: Faith, e'en with losing his wits.

Language can only reveal its own rules; a study of language teaches us language-games; it cannot give us an explanation of experience.

Seeing Yorick's skull makes Hamlet utter the gruesome conjuration: 'Now get you to my lady's chamber, and tell her, let her paint an inch thick, to this favour she must come'. Even such wallowing in bitter truth is not sufficient for him. Having observed that politicians and lawyers, creating laws of the land to preserve the form of order, are not themselves preserved, no more than a court jester, Hamlet turns to history, that other illusion of Time and human existence with its vivid imagery of emperors and battles, the greed for patches of ground, a language with its pretension to incontestable facts:

> Alexander died, Alexander was buried, Alexander returneth to dust; the dust is earth; of earth we make loam; and why of that loam whereto he was converted might they not stop a beer barrel?

The great Alexander is reduced to a mere name, a word signifying nothing of history, and the idea of history is mocked by a boyish jingle:

> Imperious Cæsar, dead and turned to clay,
> Might stop a hole to keep the wind away.

Of course, much of the Clown's black humour and Hamlet's easy philosophising perform other functions in the play: Hamlet's return has to be established and the idea suggested that his recent experience at sea, where he has been involved in mortal struggle, has reconciled him to life: his language is now cynical and mocking and not the earlier anguished one demanding answers; the graveside humour and contemplation of skulls is also setting up the scene to effect the greatest dramatic impact and to extract the maximum irony from Ophelia's present burial; but the dialogue has insisted that one note not only the meaning of the words spoken but the idea of Language itself: without the idea of law and history and their relationship with the language on which each is founded, which idea serves as a metaphor for the relationship between reality and language, Hamlet's speeches on seeing the skulls would be trite and serve no purpose than the rather easy one of dramatic irony.

*

Who is Osric? We have not seen him before and suddenly he appears in the final scene of the play as if he were a long-established courtier. Horatio has not heard of him and Hamlet describes Osric to him in the most contemptuous terms, in an aside:

> He hath much land, and fertile. Let a beast be lord of beasts, and his crib shall stand at the king's mess. 'Tis a chough, but, as I say, spacious in the possession of dirt.

The phrase *much land, and fertile* is a contrast with *a little patch of ground* which is barren; and *spacious in the possession of dirt* places Osric firmly among the skulls in the graveyard.

It soon appears that Osric is a dandy, a 'wit' given to florid, euphuistic speech, a lover of superfluous words; he is a caricature of an intelligent human being, the very opposite of Hamlet, impressing his listeners with what he no doubt believes is a refined and an elegant vocabulary but in fact is only a pretentious one; he represents the perversion of an intellectual, for language in his mouth is not a medium of expressing ideas but has become mere decoration, all surface glitter like his clothes and quite empty underneath. The gift of language is reduced to glibness and, as with his hat, Osric cannot put it to its 'right use'. He is a hypocrite, too, agreeing with Hamlet that it is cold and then that it is sultry and hot. When Osric gives a verbose description of Laertes, Hamlet mocks him with his, Osric's, inflated language:

> Sir, his definement suffers no perdition in you, though, I know, to divide him inventorially would dozy th' arithmetic of memory, and yet but yaw neither in respect of his quick sail. But, in the verity of extolment, I take him to be a soul of great article, and his infusion of such dearth and rareness as, to make true diction of him, his semblable is his mirror, and who else would trace him, his umbrage, nothing more.

In fact, Hamlet out-Osrics Osric in this passage, thus creating a devastating parody of a speech which is already a parody of civilised language. Horatio is bewildered by it and says, 'Is't not possible to understand in another tongue?' Hamlet has taken his verbal revenge, however, and in the process exhausted much of Osric's vocabulary, for Horatio says in an aside to Hamlet: 'His purse is empty already. All's golden words are spent.'

We reach line 176 of the scene before Osric goes. The message was a simple one: Hamlet is invited to fight a duel with Laertes and that the King has laid a bet on the fight. By contrast to this extravagant scene, soon after Osric has left, a Lord enters with another message from the King, delivers it prosaically within a few lines and exits. The contrast is so deliberately created that one is obliged to look again at Osric and ponder his significance. An extreme decadence of speech (as well as his exaggeratedly foppish appearance) marks him out too conspicuously for him not to be a symbolic representation of so-called civilised man given to a portentous speech which, however, once we examine his seemingly extraordinary combinations of words, is as poor in ideas as it seems rich in vocabulary; and his civilised appearance is only that, an appearance, for he is truly a beast, no more.

We are seeing, too, in the figure of Osric, what Hamlet might easily have become, a popular, 'witty' courtier charming everyone with his pretty speeches, one who never questions the emptiness of his trendy words. Osric's language emphasises the idea of the failure of language, and Hamlet, bitterly mocking Osric, is spitting out a frenzy of worthless words, because he has very nearly reached a point where he must reject language and embrace silence.

A mood of resignation seems to have come over Hamlet, though his mind continues to play with verbal formulae – 'If it be now, 'tis not to come; if it be not to come, it will be now; if it be not now, yet it will come'. It is as if he wished to exhaust the possibilities of mathematical combinations of the same old words to see if there is not a combination yet to be discovered which might not be the formula of revelation. To this juggling of words, Hamlet adds, 'Let be'. These two words are spoken softly, resignedly, as if he were dismissing all propositions out of his mind, and are possibly drowned by the trumpets and drums which announce the arrival of the King, the Queen and 'all the State', and one is distracted from noticing that that 'Let be' is Hamlet's final statement before the dramatic events of the last scene overtake him with their unstoppable force and that 'Let be' is, of course, the resolution in his mind of that debate in which 'To be, or not to be' was one proposition, a key one, of which to test the implications.

Now he realises that life offers no alternative but to let be, for the events will overtake us, absorbing us in their riotous unpredictability: no amount of contemplation and the probing of language will stifle the loud trumpets which replace the ideas of life with a pageant of the living. But even in his resolution to accept action, Hamlet is driven by the habits of his mind, and asking Laertes to pardon him, says:

> Was't Hamlet wronged Laertes? Never Hamlet.
> If Hamlet from himself be ta'en away,
> And when he's not himself does wrong Laertes,
> Then Hamlet does it not, Hamlet denies it.
> Who does it then? His madness. If't be so,
> Hamlet is of the faction that is wronged;
> His madness is poor Hamlet's enemy.

It is a passage in which he has reduced his own behaviour to a verbal formula, making his own name into an object (just as he had earlier with 'Alexander').

They prepare to commence the duel and the King ceremoniously makes a grandiose speech – 'Set me the stoops of wine upon the table'.

And let the kettle to the trumpet speak,
The trumpet to the cannoneer without,
The cannons to the heavens, the heaven to earth . . .

The trumpet speak. And let there be such a thunderous noise that his own lies may be drowned in a violent elimination of silence, that state in which humans are liable to ponder meanings or to which they are reduced when all attempts at meaning have been exhausted. But the King loses in this final attempt to camouflage his own evil intention, and the sounds which command attention when the King, the Queen and Laertes are lying dead on the stage are the words of Hamlet's dying voice:

O, I could tell you –
But let it be.

There is more anguish in that *could tell* than is due to the frustration of not having time to explain himself, and he asks Horatio to 'tell my story': he himself cannot explain himself and sinks into a final silence.

Fortinbras, whose business in this world has been like Alexander's, to go about conquering a little patch of ground, enters a moment after Hamlet dies and this is the first time we see him at the court in Elsinore. Four members of Denmark's nobility lie dead before him in a vivid metaphor, reducing the court to another worthless little patch of ground, with death the dominant reality to be perceived upon it, but Fortinbras is not one given to observing ironies or even meaning, for he sees the devastation as his 'fortune' – 'For me, with sorrow I embrace my fortune'. Before doing so, he makes a token gesture in a rhetorical language:

O proud Death,
What feast is toward in thine eternal cell
That thou so many princes at a shot
So bloodily hast struck?

Horatio proposes to 'speak to th' yet unknowing world / How these things came about', and when Fortinbras declares that he is the rightful heir to the throne, Horatio responds, 'Of that I shall have also cause to speak'. As in the beginning of the play, so now in its concluding lines the word *speak* is repeatedly uttered. Fortinbras, whose mind comprehends only the imagery of action, inflicts upon the dead Hamlet the role of a soldier which he never was in life:

> Let four captains
> Bear Hamlet like a soldier to the stage . . .

and if this is not sufficient irony, Fortinbras unwittingly gives us more:

> and for his passage
> The soldiers' music and the rites of war
> Speak loudly for him.

Speak loudly. But no longer in words. At the conclusion of the first of the great tragedies, which has witnessed the failure of language, the audience is forced to hear not words but, in response to the play's final line spoken by Fortinbras ('Go, bid the soldiers shoot'), cannon being fired; the cannon, however, is being put to an empty, ceremonial use, much like Osric's words; and the noise the audience hears is an example of a writer's intellect making an imaginative, an intuitive, leap, and arriving at the symbolic meaning of actions that have still to be rehearsed and performed: the noise of the cannon with which *Hamlet* ends is the *sound and fury* of *Macbeth*, the final tragedy: it signifies *nothing*.

Othello: The Beast With Two Backs

Although he is almost exclusively the subject of the dialogue in the first scene of the play, Othello is not once mentioned in it by name. It is not till line 40, when Iago refers to *the Moor*, that one has any idea of who the third person is that Iago and Roderigo have been talking about so animatedly, and even then the idea purchased by the mind is a general one of a racial type and not of an individual.

The first part of the scene, before Desdemona's father, Brabantio, appears at a window, concerns Iago's anger at Othello for having preferred Cassio over himself to promote as his lieutenant more than it is with portraying the Moor's character; while a picture does begin to form itself of Othello, what is seen of him, including Roderigo's reference to him as 'the thick-lips', is either vague or inaccurate. The scene's emphasis is on the disgruntled Iago, and it is his character which is more roundly established. One senses the seriousness of his threat, 'Were I the Moor, I would not be Iago', and hears a coldly calculating menace in his 'I am not what I am', the concluding words of a speech in which he announces the method by which he intends to gain his 'peculiar end'. He is going to practise deception by manipulating outward appearances.

He incites Roderigo to rouse Desdemona's father and instructs him on how to create fear and outrage – 'Make after him, poison his delight . . .' – in order to gain his own end. But Roderigo's attempt at uttering a calculatedly provocative speech is pathetically futile, for all he can do is to call aloud, 'What, ho, Brabantio! Signior Brabantio, ho!'; therefore, Iago steps in and shouts,

> Awake! What, ho, Brabantio! Thieves! thieves! thieves!

> Look to your house, your daughter, and your bags!
> Thieves! thieves!

Iago's words, threatening what the prosperous merchant holds most dear, bring Brabantio to the window. When he demands what the matter is for 'this terrible summons', Roderigo's reply is ineffective and again Iago has to step in. He does so with a graphic and an obscene image, for after telling Brabantio that he has been robbed, he adds in a voice which, stressing with increasing emphasis the repeated *now*, urgently conveys the sort of warning Brabantio cannot ignore:

> Even now, now, very now, an old black ram
> Is tupping your white ewe.

Roderigo's next three attempts to communicate a sense of urgency to Brabantio are also ineffective, and Iago shouts to keep alive in Brabantio's mind the image calculated most to fill him with loathing. When Brabantio, hearing a vile statement that his daughter is coupling with a beast, asks, 'What profane wretch art thou?' Iago answers:

> I am one, sir, that comes to tell you your daughter and the Moor are now making the beast with two backs.

Again, Iago's use of *now* adds a vivid immediacy to the graphic image, no doubt creating as live action in Brabantio's mind what to him must be a loathsome act. Roderigo is inspired to make a longer speech and Iago's directness emboldens him to talk of 'the gross clasps of a lascivious Moor', a phraseology that is timid and generalised in its depiction of sexuality and serves to highlight the shocking vividness and particularity with which Iago represents the sexual act. Having made his accusations anonymously, Iago withdraws, leaving Brabantio to lament the loss of his daughter to Roderigo, in which dialogue the theme of deceiving appearances is hinted at when Brabantio says:

> Fathers, from hence trust not your daughters' minds
> By what you see them act.

He finds it hard to believe that his daughter has voluntarily eloped with the Moor and wonders whether she is not the victim of some enchantment, some black magic that creates a false picture of reality.

The first scene, then, reveals nothing of the character of Othello and the idea of him as a gifted soldier whose service Venice values is suggested only briefly towards the end of the scene and that, too, in a language which is not imagistically memorable: Iago remarks that he knows that the state needs Othello for the Cyprus wars because

> Another of his fathom they have none
> To lead their business;

– which abstract language does not make an immediate impact upon one's imagination as do the phrases concerning the black ram tupping the white ewe and the two-backed beast; even Roderigo's 'lascivious Moor' is comparatively sensational. So that the emphasis of the scene can therefore be said to be not so much upon Othello's military genius as upon Iago's portrayal of his satyriasis. The image that Iago is determined that Brabantio see is that of his fair white daughter being sexually crushed by the black Moor:

> . . . you'll have your daughter covered with a Barbary horse; you'll have your nephews neigh to you; you'll have coursers for cousins, and gennets for germans.

– meaning that Brabantio can expect his daughter to present him with a colourful motley of grand-children. Iago is appealing to a base racial instinct in Brabantio, and it is an idea that is re-inforced by Roderigo telling Brabantio that his daughter 'hath made a gross revolt'. The image emphasised by the scene is of a sexually potent Moor stooped over an innocent, though willing, white girl in a violently agitated sexual embrace.

Perhaps it is no more than a device to create a sensation in the opening minutes of the play; or perhaps, after the shock of the sexual images, the contrast presented by Othello's appearance as a well-mannered and gentle human being makes him dramatically all the more interesting and renders him even more appealing in Act I, scene iii, when he defends himself against Brabantio's charge of corrupting and stealing his daughter, a scene which leaves no doubt that in Othello we are looking at a man of honour, nobility and distinction. But the bestial sexual imagery in the opening scene is important, and it is more than a device with which to bait the audience's attention. In the final scene of the play, Desdemona will be in bed and Othello will come to her, and the audience will see a scene more shocking than the tupping of a white ewe by a black ram: it will witness the real beast with two backs.

Othello makes his first appearance in the play's second scene, standing in attentive silence – which he breaks very briefly, only to say, "Tis better as it is' – while Iago gives a lengthy self-serving account of his encounter with Brabantio and tries to impress upon Othello the danger he may expect from the powerfully influential Brabantio.

'Tis better as it is. Othello's short phrase that punctuates Iago's sixteen-line speech seems unremarkable but is in fact a statement of considerable relevance to his relationship with Iago. If only Iago were to leave everything *as it is*, Othello's fate would be a far different one. The little phrase also carries a metaphysical relevance. Brabantio's remark in the first scene ('Fathers, from hence trust not your daughters' minds / By what you see them act') had suggested that appearances can be deceptive; and now Othello's little phrase is affirming a desire for things to be as they are, which is to say the phrase is expressing the hope that reality remain as it is – that is, as it appears to be, uncorrupted by illusion and unthreatened by the doubt that it might not be what it is.

Othello is a military man, used to adversaries who appear as such; Iago is about to provide him with an enemy made up entirely of insubstantial ideas.

But immediately in the scene, what is observed of Othello is the unthreatened, imperturbable man. Advised by Iago to hide himself from the approaching Brabantio and his armed attendants, Othello says with great dignity and poise:

> Not I; I must be found.
> My parts, my title, and my perfect soul
> Shall manifest me rightly.

This early reference to his 'perfect soul' is of considerable relevance to what is to follow; these lines not only anticipate 'It is the cause, it is the cause, my soul!' of the final Act but are also related to some of the intervening imagery. It is not Brabantio but only Cassio and some officers who arrive, summoning the Moor to the Duke on the business of Cypress. Othello withdraws briefly, and Iago exploits the moment to revive the sexual imagery by informing Cassio that Othello 'to-night hath boarded a land carack', thus creating in the mind of the audience the idea of deceiving appearances: Othello has just been seen to be a man of honour and discretion and here is Iago insinuating that he is an opportunist, for apart from the sexual implication of 'boarded' there is also the idea of obtaining treasure.

Just as Othello returns, Brabantio arrives with his men and a fight ensues between them and Cassio's officers. Othello stops them and demands an explanation from Brabantio. The incensed Brabantio hurls at him a speech of offensive vituperation, accusing him of having enchanted his daughter. While his meaning is perfectly direct, that Othello must have exercised some magic over her in order to make her go against her nature, Brabantio's language has another dimension to it that has a relevance to what is beginning to appear as a philosophical current behind the unfolding action.

> For I'll refer me to all things of sense,
> If she in chains of magic were not bound,

are the opening phrases of a long, eight-line sentence in which Brabantio says of his 'tender, fair, and happy' daughter that she has been so opposed to marriage that she has rejected wealthy, handsome Venetians, and therefore it is inconceivable that she can have run of her own free will to 'the sooty bosom' of so alien a type as Othello. Brabantio merely wishes to state that he refuses to accept as truth the facts that have been presented to him, but what the words 'I'll refer me to all things of sense' are also saying is: all phenomena will need to be re-examined if what was believed to have been true about Desdemona is shown to have been false, for if the deceptive appearance of things is not caused by some magic spell then one's shock that reality is not what one had been looking at is so great that no thing that appears before the senses can go unexamined. Brabantio continues:

> Judge me the world if 'tis not gross in sense
> That thou has practised on her with foul charms,
> Abused her delicate youth with drugs or minerals
> That weaken motion.

Here too the reference is more than to the changed perception of Desdemona whose father is insisting that she is the victim of mind-altering drugs, for apart from the delicate ambiguity in the first line there is implied in the statement an acknowledgement of perception being vulnerable to deception. Brabantio's final accusation is that Othello is 'an abuser of the world, a practicer / Of arts inhibited' – which seems an extravagant charge to level against a person who has abducted one's daughter, but, surely, 'an abuser of the world' is a precise description of a person whose action makes one doubt one's conception of the world and thereby threatens a whole structure of established values.

The idea of deceiving appearances is taken up also at the beginning of the next scene (I, iii) in which the Duke and the senators are assembled to discuss the Turkish threat to Cyprus. They have been receiving inconsistent news about the Turkish fleet, and a messenger arrives to report that the Turks are making for Rhodes – that is, not to Cyprus. The Duke wonders about this change, and a senator declares, 'This cannot be', for it is against reason. He uses a brilliant image to make his point:

> 'Tis a pageant
> To keep us in false gaze.

So much of life is precisely that, be it the recounting of a myth, the acceptance of a religion, the contemplation of a philosophy, the making of astronomical observations, or be it sitting in a theatre and watching a play entitled *Othello*. With a greater or lesser degree of absorption – though, unlike the Turkish fleet, the images constituted before us may not be placed there with a deliberate design to deceive – we but gaze at a pageant and more often than not remain in a fine ecstasy of distraction, arriving at convictions that become transformed into dogma when all we have done has been to interpret a scene that has been only partially or imperfectly or misleadingly glimpsed, and the truth we believe we have thus established is rarely more than a confirmation of a previously rooted way of seeing.

When Othello arrives, the Duke greets him as 'Valiant Othello'. It is the first time the name is heard on the stage; the designation, creating so different a portrait from the lascivious Moor of the first scene, confirms how easily one can be drawn into a false gaze.

Brabantio, coming to the Duke and the senators at their emergency council of war in the middle of the night, insists that his own sorrow at losing his daughter is more urgent a business than the Ottoman threat to the state. A man of unshakable belief in the rightness of his racial prejudice, jealously guarding his possessions, he perfectly represents the universal bourgeois materialist. He declares to the Duke that his daughter 'is abused, stol'n from me, and corrupted' by magic and drugs, maintaining that it would be for nature 'prepost'rously to err' had she gone of her own choice. The Duke, not knowing that Othello is being charged, responds that the person will be answerable to the law even if he were his own son – thus setting up a nice incidental dramatic tension, for he has a moment earlier announced the employment of Othello against the enemy. Brabantio answers: 'Here is the man – this Moor', and surely the contemptuous tone in which *this Moor* is spoken contrasts strongly with the ingratiating tone that had welcomed *Valiant Othello* a few moments earlier.

Before Othello can respond to the Duke's question of what he has to say to the charge, Brabantio quickly interjects, 'Nothing, but this is so'. He is not prepared to admit any doubt; reality is what he has described it to be, and for him there can be no question of it being different in the slightest degree.

Othello begins his defence in the gentle tone of a man of good reason, using a direct, almost pedestrian speech:

> That I have ta'en away this old man's daughter,
> It is most true; true I have married her.

He insists upon the appearance being true; for him a fact is a fact, it is incontestably there, it is indisputable and final. Brabantio, however, cannot accept his version. He repeats his obsessive idea that it would be unnatural of his daughter to love the Moor:

> It is a judgment maimed and most imperfect
> That will confess perfection so could err
> Against all rules of nature . . .

Any idea that he finds repugnant is to be excluded from

existence. As earlier, Brabantio's language suggests a dimension other than his petty-minded paternalism. His is a fanatical conservatism. For him, the rules of nature are fixed and eternal.

The Duke correctly states that to make an assertion is not to give proof, and Othello is invited to continue his defence. His long speech – containing the memorable lines

> She loved me for the dangers I had passed,
> And I loved her that she did pity them

– and Desdemona's appearance and testimony convince the Duke that Brabantio's charges are false, and he returns to the affairs of state. Othello must that very night sail away to Cyprus. Desdemona requests that she accompany her husband, and Othello supports her request. Anticipating that it will be thought inappropriate and distracting for a man on a military mission to be accompanied by a young wife, Othello makes a remarkable observation:

> . . . I therefore beg it not
> To please the palate of my appetite,
> Not to comply with heat – the young affects
> In me defunct . . .

Is he saying that he is too old to be interested in sex? Or is he, like the Turks, creating a pageant to evoke a false gaze? Later in the scene, Iago says that he himself is twenty-eight years old; that might be a clue to Othello's age, for Iago's master is presumably significantly his senior. But the question of Othello's precise age is irrelevant; what is to the point is the image created by his observation. A man not young enough, or not passionate enough, to be distracted by sexual heat is certainly not the black ram tupping the white ewe that was so sensational an image in the first scene. The speech continues for ten more lines, with Othello making such an emphatic statement about the unlikelihood of his private pleasure interfering with the 'serious and great business' of the state that one would think he had undertaken the administration of a monastery. The Duke stops the amazing declaration of Othello's sexual frugality with

> Be it as you shall privately determine,
> Either for her stay or going.

The state business concluded, the Duke addresses this parting statement to Brabantio:

> And, noble signior,
> If virtue no delighted beauty lack,
> Your son-in-law is far more fair than black.

This seems at first a just remark, but it is also a nice joke at Brabantio's expense which the other senators, knowing well their colleague's fanatical conservatism, are quietly going to relish; and, of course, the remark can also be related to the theme of deceiving appearances. Brabantio, in fact, re-states that theme a line later, in the more famous couplet that has the fearful ring of a malediction:

> Look to her, Moor, if thou hast eyes to see:
> She has deceived her father, and may thee.

Roderigo, whose hopes of winning Desdemona's favours seem completely shattered, says to Iago with whom he is left alone in the concluding part of the scene that he will drown himself. Iago realises that he must devise a new strategy if he is to take his revenge against Othello, and counsels Roderigo to go to Cyprus and leads him to believe that he can expect to enjoy Desdemona. Iago reasons with Roderigo in a language that has a larger interest in the play.

'Our bodies are our gardens to the which our wills are gardeners', says Iago, stating an opening premise to an idea he goes on to develop at length. It is our will that chooses to have the garden 'sterile with idleness or manured with industry'. The idea of making the soil fertile is associated with sexuality (for which Iago's image of manure is suggestive, almost as if he held it in abomination); and sexuality, he would have us conclude, would keep human beings thoughtlessly copulating if it remained unchecked by cooling reason.

> If the balance of our lives had not one scale of reason to poise another of sensuality, the blood and baseness of our natures would conduct us to most preposterous conclusions.

Without reason, 'our carnal stings, our unbitted lusts' would keep us shaped as the two-backed beast. Iago insists that carnality is nothing but an animalistic instinct, and he is dismissive of the idea of love as professed a few minutes earlier by Desdemona in her plea to the Duke and the senators. What she has called love is to Iago 'a violent commencement in her', and as for Othello, 'The food that to him now is as luscious as locusts shall be to him shortly as bitter as coloquintida'. Iago acknowledges only the force of sexual attraction that is inevitably of a short duration, for as the fruit will turn bitter in Othello's mouth so shall Desdemona be 'sated with his body'.

Roderigo is persuaded that there is hope for him yet, and exits. In the soliloquy which concludes the first act, Iago expresses the startling suspicion that his wife has been seduced by Othello:

> I hate the Moor;
> And it is thought abroad that 'twixt my sheets
> H'as done my office.

One notes here that his expression of hatred for Othello coincides with a sexual image in his mind where the two ideas are expressed in one sentence. The suspicion is enough for him to wish to be revenged, for he is prepared to react to an appearance of a thing without demanding that it be a proved reality; this line of thinking suggests to him the scheme 'to abuse Othello's ear' with the notion that Cassio 'is too familiar with his wife'. Iago observes:

> The Moor is of a free and open nature
> That thinks men honest that but seem to be so;

the theme of deceiving appearances is here re-stated for the final time in the first Act and it is connected with the theme of sexuality. An explosive illumination seems to take place in Iago's mind:

> I have't! It is engend'red! Hell and night
> Must bring this monstrous birth to the world's light.

Iago's 'monstrous birth' refers to the idea just born in his mind, that he will lead Othello by the nose as one does an ass and make him believe that Cassio has seduced Desdemona; but the imaginative force of the phrase *this monstrous birth*, spoken just as the curtain is about to fall on the first Act, relates the idea to the images of bestial sexuality in the Act's opening scene, so that in a moment of shocking intuition one recognises another idea – that the beast with two backs gives birth to a monster. And since a birth implies life, therefore life itself is monstrous (in the sense of being unbearable or insupportable or terrible as in 'That's a monstrous idea'), being the product of 'Hell and night'. The phrase is also a reference to what is about to be shown in the scene that follows, an idea of crucial mythic significance to the larger drama.

Act II opens with Montano, the governor of Cyprus, and two Gentlemen looking out on the ocean in expectation of Othello's arrival, and the first image is that of the primeval ocean, a vast heaving mass of water, 'a high-wrought flood' on which to be seen is 'Nothing at all'. There is such a wind that the stormy ocean seems to be swelling up to the sky, the 'wind-shaked surge' is rising up to the North Star in a universe throbbing turbulently in its original chaos, containing Nothing.

We are looking at the earth-encircling ocean and at that primeval water which in universal myths is the symbol for the creative force. In that vast abstraction of water, in a 'foul and violent tempest', is the ship carrying Othello to Cyprus, with 'Great Jove' beseeched to 'swell his sail' with his divine and life-giving 'pow'rful breath'. We are looking, too, at the hero's journey by ship, the hero who is swallowed by the sea monster and must be delivered through ritual sacrifice.

The ships transporting Cassio, Iago and Desdemona arrive before Othello's, and in what appears to be a routine creation of dramatic tension the hero's arrival is delayed, arousing the fear that the hero might have died during the voyage. But the imaginative structure shaping the ideas behind the language is far from routine. One observes the precise parallels with mythological images – and this scene is a perfect example of the creative imagination unconsciously seizing upon universal and timeless symbols through which to depict a living human drama.* To emerge from the sea monster, the mythic hero lights a fire within the monster's belly, transforms the womb of death to the womb of life and is cast upon the shore. These images are almost precisely duplicated in *Othello*. Cassio, appealing to Great Jove, prays that Othello's ship 'bless this bay', that Othello 'Make love's quick pants in Desdemona's arms', and 'Give renewed fire to our extincted spirits'. When Othello arrives, he makes straight for Desdemona's arms and soon exclaims:

> O my soul's joy!
> If after every tempest come such calms,
> May the winds blow till they have wakened death!

* Cf. C. G. Jung, *Symbols of Transformation*, London, 1956, p. 347, to observe a striking affinity of imagery between Jung's description of the 'worldwide myth' and Shakespeare's rendering of this scene.

It is as if he himself has been wakened from death and that his sea voyage has been a passage to some nether world, for the Desdemona whom he embraces is more than his worldly wife, becoming in these lines a projection of Othello's own self or has become that womb in which the journeying soul discovers its real self.

At the literal level, Othello's delay not only makes for dramatic tension but also creates the occasion to further the plot by bringing Cassio and Desdemona together and then producing a dialogue between Desdemona and Iago which is witty and plays amusingly with paradox and, because the audience is privy to Iago's design, is touched with menace. Even in these seemingly playful lines, there is a reference to the themes established earlier. Desdemona's passing remark – 'I am not merry; but I do beguile / The thing I am by seeming otherwise' – is hardly necessary in the context but it does serve to remind one of the idea of deceptive appearances, and Iago's talk is so coloured by sexual innuendoes, and echoes his more graphic images in the first Act, that at the conclusion of the dialogue Desdemona says of him to Cassio, 'Is he not a most profane and liberal [that is, licentious] counsellor?' But this part of the scene, which prolongs the tension even as it relieves it with witty dialogue, serves also to heighten the imaginative effect of the hero's deliverance from the ocean, for we hold in an oppressive suspense the image created earlier of 'The wind-shaked surge, with high and monstrous mane' – the image of the sea monster – and experience a profound sense of release from oppression when Othello reappears and, embracing Desdemona, declares:

> It gives me wonder great as my content
> To see you here before me. O my soul's joy!

His language in this speech is poetical, his meaning metaphysical. This is a very different language from what was heard from Othello in the first Act where he confessed 'Rude am I in my speech' (I, iii, 81) and had gone on to announce

> And little of this great world can I speak
> More than pertains to feats of broil and battle;

when he explained himself to the Duke and the senators, he was pedestrian and matter-of-fact; sometimes he affected a martial tone, and his only poetically memorable words were the two lines 'She loved me for the dangers I had passed, / And I loved her that she did pity them'. Now, after the sea voyage, he is intensely poetical.

Still in Desdemona's embrace, he says:

> If it were now to die,
> 'Twere now to be most happy; for I fear
> My soul hath her content so absolute
> That not another comfort like to this
> Succeeds in unknown fate.

The perfect bliss that Othello speaks of is the soul's; he makes no reference to the body. When he says of kissing Desdemona, 'And this, and this, the greatest discords be', the idea conveyed is that some ultimate music, some perfect harmony is created by their conjoined bodies, a music of such transcendental beauty that it cannot be heard and the only discord that is audible is when their kissing lips make a little smacking sound when very briefly they part. Since no more absolute bliss is to be expected from the future, therefore the present one is the extent of what paradise can have to offer: from which it must follow that to experience this particular bliss is to be in paradise. 'I cannot speak enough of this content', Othello says, using the word 'content' for the third time in twelve lines, so overwhelmed is he by the indescribable experience. It is a condition in which the body is an irrelevance; at most, the human frame is a receptacle for ecstasy, for it is the 'soul's joy' which is the overpowering experience. To speak of the soul's 'content so absolute' that there can be no happiness superior to it and to be possessed by 'too much of joy' that no words can be spoken to describe it is also to give definition to the abstraction denoted by the word *love*. The image being presented of this love is the male and the female so conjoined that they are like one melody – which is also a sound made by breath, and breath, in turn, is a metaphor for divine inspiration – a pure and marvellous abstraction that, while it is visible as the essence of beauty, is not seen and, being heard as divine music, is inaudible. It is a sexual union in which the bodies dissolve one into the other and from that union is born the idea of a perfect love. This is a sexuality that has no connection with any regenerative function, for the object of the union is the 'soul's joy'; it is a sexuality which assumes that innocence has an integrity that cannot be corrupted, for the united male and female wish to experience a combined death in the moment of their supreme bliss – which is to say, they are resolved to exclude a third person from making a sensual contact with their own living flesh. That surely is the force of Othello's 'If it were now to die, / 'Twere now to be most happy'. Delivered from the ocean, he has entered that ultimate purity of light which is the blinding vision associated with spiritual ecstasy.

But standing beside this harmonious image is Iago for whom the union takes the shape of the beast with two backs, and it is not surprising that Othello's beautiful poetical structuring of love should receive a cynical aside from Iago, who remarks, 'O, you are well tuned now!' Othello's concept of love is idealistic and is associated with the soul's possession of an absolute content; in this concept, woman is idealised and the man's desire is not for an animalistic sexual union with her but for that physical dissolution within her which is a harmony so perfect it is a spiritual ecstasy – the continuation, that is, of the soul's absolute content; this complete transcendental happiness depends upon the perfection of the idealised woman, which is to say, her physical purity, for she must be like some divine light unstained even by a speck of a shadow, or she must be like a harmony in which there is no discord; therefore, if there is the remotest suggestion that this ideal woman has been sexually united with another man then the whole concept of the soul's absolute content collapses.

Othello's suffering will come not so much from the experience of jealousy that another man has seduced his wife as from the collapse of the ideal vision which he had experienced in that enchanted moment when having survived the sea monster he arrived upon that shore which momentarily gave him the experience of perfect bliss associated with spiritual content. The female's presumed union with another man pollutes the purity of that vision as though what had been pure light is now filled with motes of dust. That original pure light of the blinding vision of his spiritual bliss will have deceived him and he himself will 'put out the light'.

Iago stays back with Roderigo in the last part of Act II, scene i and one notes that after Othello's poetical language about his soul's joy Iago is made to talk directly in the plainest prose about everyday sex. As he had earlier, he talks of sexuality as a base, animalistic instinct. He has certainly seen what humanity is about. He says of Desdemona that when her 'blood is made dull with the act of sport, there should be, again to inflame it and to give satiety a fresh appetite, loveliness in favour, sympathy in years, manners, and beauties; all which the Moor is defective in'. His analysis of human psychology and of the vanity of human wishes is flawless. He might, incidentally, even be correct in saying that Othello won Desdemona by 'bragging and telling her fantastical lies'. His immediate object in speaking so plainly is to provoke the dull Roderigo to make him serve Iago's desire for revenge, but the juxtaposition of Othello's and Iago's contrasting ideas about sex is surely a poignant one. Othello has arrived at a stage that is beyond ordinary life: after his deliverance from the ocean he is in a state of pure being – or is possessed by a delusion of it – that demands he believe the body that he has projected as his soul's joy be absolutely unstained; Iago's belief is rooted in base reality and he is contemptuous of life (which is why, for example, he can kill his wife without a moment's thought even though she can do him no further harm). Iago may be the incarnation of the devil engineering the consigning of Othello's soul to hell, but he certainly can be seen as the opponent of any grand religious concept of life that proposes for the soul a future of beatific bliss; his several references to sexuality in a language that debases the act is a perfect antithesis to sexuality as a transcendental experience. He will 'abuse Othello's ears' with precisely this imagery, suggesting to him that his soul's joy and his lieutenant have been going at it 'as prime as goats, as hot as monkeys'. He will so change Othello's perception that, granted one more opportunity to see his soul's light, he will extinguish it.

Most pointedly, Iago is given a soliloquy at the end of the scene; in it, he restates an earlier idea, that he suspects Othello of having slept with his, Iago's, wife; to this he adds another suspicion, that Cassio has also seduced Emilia. This could be Iago's own fantasy, an idea engendered by his psychological necessity to believe in the righteousness of his evil plot against Othello. But be that as it may, what is significant is Iago's language. Saying that Othello 'Hath leaped into my seat', he phrases his need for revenge thus:

> And nothing can or shall content my soul
> Till I am evened with him, wife for wife;

These lines are spoken, about five minutes later, in the very same scene in which Othello has said, 'My soul hath her content so absolute'; Othello's language, as we have seen, was concerned with a metaphysical idea; Iago is concerned only with the physical, the immediate gross body and the base passions with which it is imbued. Iago's 'content my soul' can be seen as an ironical comment upon Othello's 'My soul hath her content'; for Iago's statement implies that content can accompany only a worldly satisfaction, whereas Othello's words implied he was in some blissful transcendental state and not in this world.

Although Othello has experienced a supreme bliss when, emerging from the ocean, he has embraced Desdemona, in fact he has not yet been joined to her in sexual intercourse, as is explicitly stated immediately after Act II, scene i. After the brief second scene in which a herald makes a proclamation calling for a festive celebration, Act II, scene iii has Othello saying to Desdemona:

> Come, my dear love.
> The purchase made, the fruits are to ensue;
> That profit's yet to come 'tween me and you.

He leads his wife away, leaving Cassio to keep guard over the festivities, counselling him 'Not to outsport discretion'. Iago now joins Cassio and says of Othello and Desdemona, 'He hath not yet made wanton the night with her, and she is sport for Jove', which sentence not only confirms Othello's statement about his unconsummated marriage but with the word *sport* also makes mockery of Othello's 'outsport' remark that is still fresh in the audience's mind. The emphatic statement that the marriage has not yet been consummated makes the metaphysical and mythological interpretation of the earlier scene all the more persuasive: Othello has not known Desdemona's body and yet his soul is possessed of an absolute content by the mere act of having his own being merged with hers, as if they were two beams of light which, coinciding in space, made a diffusion of luminosity in which physical matter could no more be discerned.

What follows in Act II, scene iii is the rapid development of Iago's plot to manipulate Cassio and Roderigo in his evil scheme. He provokes a brawl that leads to Montano being wounded by Cassio, and manipulates the return of Othello so that he may witness Cassio's guilt and dismiss him from his service. Achieving this, Iago then persuades Cassio to petition Desdemona to re-instate him in Othello's favour, so that Iago can find the occasion to create a circumstantial evidence of Desdemona's infidelity. It is a deftly handled, fast-paced scene, with a lot of absorbing action and dramatic tension; though several of the speeches are in prose, the language is still charged with poetical force, and there are imagistic references to the play's larger themes. Most significant of these are Cassio's statements after he has been dismissed by Othello. Lamenting the loss of his reputation, he says, 'I have lost the immortal part of myself, and what remains is bestial'; a little later, berating the power of wine to make us lose our reason, he bitterly remarks how we 'transform ourselves into beasts'; and then comes to this conclusion: 'To be now a sensible man, by and by a fool, and presently a beast!'.

He leaves after he has been comforted by Iago with the hope that Desdemona will listen favourably to his petition and represent his cause to her husband; and now Iago, excited that he has his victims where he wants them, says that when Desdemona

> pleads strongly to the Moor,
> I'll pour this pestilence into his ear,
> That she repeals him for her body's lust;

Invariably referring to the body as corrupt flesh, here Iago's declaration combines two themes in one sentence: the idea of base sexuality is stated immediately after the expression concerning falsehood, or the creation of a deceiving appearance. Cassio's statements about sensible men transforming themselves into beasts, and especially his image of 'the immortal part' of the self that is counterpointed to the 'bestial' part, are connected to the play's earlier imagery, of Othello's contented soul, his immortal part, and Iago's beast with two backs, the bestial part.

The remaining three acts of the play bring to a resolution these themes of the soul's journey, the base nature of sexuality, and the deceptive appearance of reality. The emphasis now is on quick action, and much of the language is without imagistic interest. For example:

> Good morrow, good lieutenant. I am sorry
> For your displeasure; but all will sure be well.

> The general and his wife are talking of it,
> And she speaks for you stoutly.
>
> (Act III, scene i)

This prosaic speech has little to distinguish it; nor is there anything remarkable in the following lines:

> I know't; I thank you. You do love my lord;
> You have known him long; and be you well assured
> He shall in strangeness stand no farther off
> Than in a political distance.
>
> (Act III, scene iii)

The first group of lines is spoken by Emilia, the second by Desdemona. There is nothing distinctive in the language to give it the mark of a particular sensibility. Similarly, Iago's words (also from Act III, scene iii):

> I am glad of this; for now I shall have reason
> To show the love and duty that I bear you
> With franker spirit. Therefore, as I am bound,
> Receive it from me. I speak not yet of proof.

Much of the last three acts of the play is composed in this kind of direct language that simply keeps the action unfolding at a fast pace. But even in this simplicity there are moments when the drama is charged with ambiguities that refer back to the imagistic structure earlier established, and when new images are introduced their power is all the greater.

There is an example in the opening of Act III, scene i of what seems to be an irrelevance taking on, when examined closely, both relevance and significance. Cassio instructs some musicians to play outside the chamber where Othello and Desdemona are asleep. The Clown comes to dismiss the musicians, makes a couple of frivolous remarks and says in conclusion, 'to hear music the general does not greatly care'.

The Clown's remarks are amusing and seem intended to provide light relief. But if one recalls again Othello's speeches on his arrival in Cyprus when he stood embracing his soul's joy, it will be remembered that he had referred to harmony so perfect that 'the greatest discords' in it were no more than the sounds made by repeated kisses and that, hearing this, Iago had said in an aside,

> O, you are well tuned now!
> But I'll set down the pegs that make this music,

so that a curse seemed to be put upon that harmony. When in Act III, scene i the musicians begin to play, the Clown's first remark to them is: 'Why, masters, ha' your instruments been in Naples, that they speak i' th' nose thus?' There are two ideas in this sentence: first, that the sound being made by the musicians is unharmonious; and, two, since the reference to Naples is an allusion to venereal disease, the sentence contains a buried image of corrupt sexuality. Furthermore, the fact that the music is being played outside the chamber in which Othello and Desdemona are presumably in each other's embrace, continuing to experience the earlier perfect harmony in their being one, therefore the musicians' noise constitutes a mocking and ironical comment and the allusion to disease brings sexuality down from its idealised elevated level, from its association with heavenly music and divine beauty, to the base common level where it is associated with filth and decay.

The Clown then gives the musicians some money and tells them: 'the general so likes your music that he desires you, for love's sake, to make no more noise with it', a remark in which the phrase *for love's sake* is exquisite both in its position in the sentence as well as for its implied irony. The lover in the bliss of his harmony or deep in his soul's joy desires not to hear the noise made by reality. He 'does not greatly care' to hear music. His ears are closed to it because he believes himself in a transcendental state. But we have already heard Iago say that he will 'abuse Othello's ears' and that he will pour 'pestilence into his ear'. The onomatopœia of Othello's 'And this, and this, the greatest discords be' that had echoed the music of his kisses shall become transformed to the hissing of the snake in his ear. He will receive knowledge that will make him doubt reality.

In Act III, scene iii, when Desdemona leaves him after having made a long plea on Cassio's behalf, Othello makes one of his most poetical statements:

> Perdition catch my soul
> But I do love thee! and when I love thee not,
> Chaos is come again.

Desdemona's speeches to him concerning Cassio have already a little soured his bliss, for she has been over-solicitous, and immediately after he makes this statement Iago enters and begins to pour his pestilence into his ear. His soul, then, is in danger of losing its joy, has indeed begun to fall, for it must be caught in a desperate act so that he can continue to believe in his love. But there is the possibility of loss and with it the return of *chaos*. It is the chaos of the primeval ocean; what returns is the memory of being in the belly of the sea monster, in the womb of death, for the failure to love is a form of death since it stifles fruitful desire, and when there is no new life then there is no life, there is only the chaos before being. As yet, Othello is holding on to the common conception of life; his sense of reality has not yet been undermined by deceptive appearances being presented to him as images of truth. Only, a doubt has entered his soul that he might yet be only in the earliest origins of his being. *Chaos is come again*. My memory of the past could well be a prescient knowledge of a future for I am in that chaos of the self where all possible alternatives of existence beam, like stars from the farthest regions of the universe, pulsations of dim, but fully recognised, images of that complex of matter which, in the shifting of the light just before a cloud overtakes the bright moon, is recognised by me, possibly as a delusion, as my unique self. Of course, this last extravagant sentence is not necessarily Othello's condition, but then, what can one say when *Chaos is come again*?

Iago has begun to abuse his ears. He says to Othello, 'Men should be what they seem', and again, 'Certain, men should be what they seem', which is a bit too obviously ironical since he himself is invariably being called honest. This is spoken almost as a deliberate provocation for he says a little later of Desdemona:

> She did deceive her father, marrying you;
> And when she seemed to shake and fear your looks,
> She loved them most.

Othello cannot deny that this was so, and Iago, seizing his advantage, empties a vial of vicious poison into his ear, saying, 'She that, so young, could give out such seeming . . .', it is enough, when Iago presently leaves him, for Othello to curse marriage and to prefer the life of a toad than to have to suffer the fate of a cuckold. Iago's statements exploit the appearance of reality, for he can refer to historical facts and convince Othello that deception was ever one of the surfaces of reality; Iago will bring to him that knowledge which will be as larger and larger doses of this same poison: *She that, so young, could give out such a seeming* – what, then, can Othello believe of reality? Already, even before Iago communicates this painful revelation, Othello is concerned about what he refers to as 'the business of my soul', that very soul which had been so contented.

When the poison has set in, Othello says:

> I had been happy if the general camp,
> Pioners and all, had tasted her sweet body,
> So I had known nothing.

That is the crucial statement: *So I had known nothing*. And there you have the great paradox of life: not to have knowledge is to be in a state of ignorant bliss or of perpetual misery; to have knowledge is to be filled with despair.

He wants to know for sure, however. He will be satisfied. Iago asks:

> . . . how satisfied, my lord?
> Would you, the supervisor, grossly gape on?
> Behold her topped?

Iago never loses an opportunity to enunciate a graphic representation of the sexual act in a language that eliminates all beauty from the performance. If the vulgarity of 'topped' is not enough, he soon makes the picture nastily bestial:

> It is impossible you should see this . . .

so that certainly not only Othello but also the audience sees perfectly well the image that he projects:

> . . . Were they as prime as goats, as hot as monkeys,
> As salt as wolves in pride, and fools as gross
> As ignorance made drunk.

With goats, monkeys and wolves joining the ram, the ewe and the Barbary horses, here is quite a zoo of copulating animals! Given this animalistic reproductive frenzy followed by Iago's fanciful rendering of Cassio's sleeping with Desdemona in an invented dream sequence which Othello is deceived into believing is a representation of a true reality, Othello can only cry, 'O monstrous, monstrous!', words that are associated with Iago's *this monstrous birth* at the end of the first Act, as he stares horror-stricken at creation which is not the soul's deliverance from the primeval chaos to a condition of supreme bliss but the body's monstrous birth that owes its origin to the beast with two backs.

Othello is convinced that Iago's suggestive insinuations concerning Cassio and Desdemona are true and falls to his knees to swear 'a sacred vow' to have his revenge 'by yond marble heaven', and Iago, hypocritically kneeling too, swears by the 'ever-burning lights above'. It is a poignantly poetical moment, the two men kneeling under the great sky which for one has a divine solidity and is the terminus of the soul's journey and for the other is 'lights' and 'elements', unknowable abstractions. Othello, resolved that both Cassio and Desdemona must die, makes his pact with the devil. Iago cruelly tempts him once more, asking that he let Desdemona live. But Othello cries aloud,

> Damn her, lewd minx! O, damn her! damn her!

His soul's joy has turned to a minx, a lewd woman, a species of dog – that is, the perfect ideal is no more than a corruptible body, love is something that can be purchased and the ensuing act is associated with another beast. Othello, by the end of Act III, scene iii is entirely convinced by Iago, to whom he says: 'Now art thou my lieutenant', which is to say, the Self has met his Other and has begun to be consumed by it.

Desdemona observes the change in Othello when, in Act III, scene iv after the dialogue concerning the handkerchief, she remarks, 'My lord is not my lord'. Emilia notices that Othello's ill-tempered behaviour could be a form of jealousy and says that in 'jealous souls'

> 'Tis a monster
> Begot upon itself, born on itself.

Startled by this forceful analysis of the self's possession by the other, Desdemona exclaims:

> Heaven keep that monster from Othello's mind!

But, of course, in the chaos that is fast becoming Othello's mind that monster has already had its birth. And the next we see of Othello, in Act IV, scene i, the first words spoken by Iago are addressed to his mind as if they were intended to nourish the monster there: 'Will you think so?', where the emphasis of the speaking voice is on *think*. And into that mind Iago introduces the provocative image, 'Or to be naked with her friend in bed', teasing the mind with speculation which it perceives as reality, and soon Othello is physically shaking and uttering words in a breathless, panting manner – 'Lie with her? lie on her? – We say lie on her when they belie her. – Lie with her! Zounds, that's fulsome. – Handkerchief – confessions – handkerchief!' – until growling like a monster he collapses in an epileptic fit. Iago, who had seen him have a similar fit on the previous day, underscores the image of the monster when he says that if Othello does not recover soon 'he foams at the mouth' and then 'Breaks out to savage madness'. And when Othello comes out of his present fit he himself says, 'A hornèd man's a monster and a beast.'

Iago now stages a scene between himself and Cassio for the concealed Othello to witness; Iago talks to Cassio about his mistress Bianca and leads Othello to understand that Cassio's answers concerning Bianca refer to Desdemona. This scene is a perfect representation of the idea of reality as a set of appearances that deceive; and since Bianca is a prostitute, for remarks about her to be identified as pertaining to Desdemona suggests the idea that base sexuality, that which makes a woman a minx, is seen to have overtaken untainted beauty, which was the soul's joy. Iago's manipulation of the scene is helped by the opportune arrival of Bianca who talks of 'that same handkerchief' and, waving it in the air, refers to it as 'some minx's token'. The scene convinces Othello that he has observed the real truth and has proof of Desdemona's guilt. He has been shown a false representation of reality and he has believed it; later in Act IV, scene i, when he strikes Desdemona before Lodovico and she is in tears, he says of her emotional state, 'O well-painted passion!', thus showing that he sees a true reality as a false one. After Iago's manipulated scene, Othello is at once determined to kill Desdemona and asks Iago to bring him some poison. Iago answers: 'Do it not with poison. Strangle her in her bed, even the bed she had contaminated'. As always, the act associated with procreation is imagined by Iago to have been something vile, and he now has succeeded in making Othello believe so. It is not merely that Desdemona must die; she must be killed in the matrimonial bed, almost as if, in keeping with his idea that sexuality is an abomination practised by unthinking animals, Iago demands the ritualistic killing of the chaste bride.

In Act IV, scene ii, Othello, wanting to be alone in the chamber with Desdemona, tells Emilia, 'Leave procreants alone and shut the door'; the reference to love-making is an ironical one since Othello's intention is to pour his fury upon Desdemona in a most vicious language in which he calls her a whore, a strumpet and a 'public commoner', words that associate the pure Desdemona with the tainted Bianca. In a longer speech, after saying that he could tolerate any extremity of affliction, be it disease or poverty or public disgrace, he states that there is one thing he cannot contemplate:

> But there where I have garnered up my heart,
> Where either I must live or bear no life,
> The fountain from the which my current runs
> Or else dries up – to be discarded thence,
> Or keep it as a cistern for foul toads
> To knot and gender in –

The central image here is of water. Othello sees his life originating from a fountain, his body a stream flowing from that source; there is an implied beauty or a sense of purity in the image of the fountain and a notion of innocent freedom to the running current; that is followed by the shock of the stream drying up and then the fearful image of the cistern; the fountain, his original home which is understood to be flowing freely and for ever, is replaced by the small, constricted and imprisoning space of the cistern; what is more, where there was pure, free-flowing water there is now a polluted puddle in which 'foul toads' are breeding themselves. The soul that had come out of the ocean and had imagined it was in possession of supreme bliss here confronts an altered reality, a confinement in filthy water in which the bodies of mindless little beasts copulate.

Desdemona is so stunned by Othello's verbal attack that at first she can scarcely speak when Emilia comes to her. Then she says:

> I cannot weep; nor answers have I none
> But what should go by water.

'But what should go by water' is a wonderfully poetical and mysterious way of saying simply, 'But tears'. The only answer she has to Emilia's question about Othello's behaviour is to shed tears but she finds herself incapable of doing so. Her phraseology suggests an unconscious awareness of the significance of water, that there is some prohibition, some malediction associated with it that temporarily blocks the flow of tears from her eyes.

Act V, scene ii, Desdemona asleep in her bed and enter Othello *with a light*. And the still flame illuminating his face, he begins his greatest speech:

> It is the cause, it is the cause, my soul.

The language of this soliloquy is divine poetry, which is perhaps appropriate, for the moment is charged with spiritual intensity. The light falling upon Othello is not only from the flame he brings to the room but is also the radiance reflecting from the chaste bride asleep in the bed upon which, following her instructions, Emilia has laid her wedding sheets, so that it is as if their wedding night were being enacted anew. To the bride comes her husband, holding up the light, thus eliminating darkness or that obscurity which confuses the mind's perception of reality. He gazes down upon her snow-white skin that is 'smooth as monumental alabaster', dazzled by the light's revelation of the unambiguous vision. He is looking at truth; before him is the potential for his soul's absolute content. But what he sees is an interpreted reality, for he who had been compelled to observe that appearances were true, now, looking at truth, is convinced he stares at merely an appearance of it. It is no more than 'the cunning'st pattern of excelling nature'. But for a moment his soul is drawn to the bride and he bends over her and kisses her. 'One more, one more!' he whispers, kissing again, and then again. The image before us is the precise rendering of Othello's statement – 'And this, and this, the greatest discords be' – that he had talked of when, after his deliverance from the ocean, he had discovered perfect harmony; indeed, 'One more, one more!' can be said to be an echo of 'And this, and this'. But now he has no belief in harmony, and his action, pursuing an earlier idealised conception of his own reality, is tragically weighted by irony, for his kisses are not a prelude to the soul's ultimate illumination by the blinding vision of achieved joy but are merely an earthly distraction before he puts out the light.

After he has smothered her and hears Emilia calling from the door, Othello says:

> Methinks it should be now a huge eclipse
> Of sun and moon. . . .

Having put out the light, he would prefer total universal darkness. The bride is killed by having her breath stopped. Breath – divine inspiration, as in Jove's 'pow'rful breath' – is the symbol for life, and by smothering the bride Othello is choking off the source of life.

In the events that rapidly follow in the same scene, Iago

suddenly kills his wife Emilia after she has spoken words that incriminate him. 'O, lay me by my mistress' side', she asks, dying. And then, presumably having been laid next to Desdemona, for Emilia speaks to her dead body ('What did thy song bode, lady?') as to one lying next to her, she tells Othello:

> Moor, she was chaste. She loved thee, cruel Moor:
> So come my soul to bliss as I speak true.

The reference to the soul's bliss, especially by being placed next to an affirmation of Desdemona's chaste love, is surely a heart-rending irony for Othello who had indeed come to his bliss and had the chance to remain in it had he only not been deceived by appearances or had he not compromised his own original sense of reality. He now hears truth. And then, after his magnificent final speech and after having seemingly surrendered his weapons he produces another one and stabs himself. He staggers towards the bed, and says:

> I kissed thee ere I killed thee. No way but this,
> Killing myself, to die upon a kiss.

The stage direction that follows states: *He falls upon the bed and dies*. He has finally come to the bridal bed to lie in it and his final kiss is the sound of discord before his soul is in eternal possession of harmony. But Emilia had earlier asked to be laid next to her mistress. Two bodies, then, lie in the bed upon which Othello falls. There lies in his marriage bed the beast with two backs. Its name is Death.

King Lear: The Bias of Nature

His nobles assembled, his two elder daughters with their husbands before him, his youngest daughter present and her two suitors sent for, Lear, King of Britain, asks for the map and, speaking in measured, deliberate tones, announces:

> Know that we have divided
> In three our kingdom;

he speaks in a language that admits of no doubt: the knowledge that he is transmitting concerning the physical world is certain: the map is in front of everyone to see. The phrase *Know that we* is spoken in a manner that implies that the listeners must receive the knowledge as incontestable fact. The choice, and positioning, of the words is significant: all that Lear seems to be saying is, 'We have divided our kingdom in three'; the words *Know that* are redundant because it is obvious that he is making an announcement or a proclamation, while the inversion which changes the simple phrase 'our kingdom in three' to 'In three our kingdom' has to be ascribed to poetical (or metrical) necessity; therefore, the functioning of the prefatory *Know that* is a rhetorical one, to create a persuasive emphasis, and since the sentence begins in the middle of a line after a cæsura, *Know* therefore bears a strong accent, requiring the emphasis upon it to be deliberate and consequently to be remarked upon by the audience. The inversion in the second part of the statement keeps in suspense the object of the division to the end, making it the final word, *kingdom*. The sentence does not end there, though one idea of it is complete – that the person speaks with assurance about his knowledge of the real world in which his own identity, that of a monarch (the supreme possessor of worldly property) is undisputed; after the brief pause, the sentence continues to express a secondary idea, that of being freed from worldly attachments in preparation for one's death.

King Lear is a play that works simultaneously at several levels; it is emotionally overwhelming and intellectually exhilarating; it saturates one with the sorrows of human suffering, successively evoking emotions of pain, tenderness, revulsion and sympathy, and amazes the mind with the range of its philosophical and psychological ideas. The preponderance of the imagery involving eyesight undoubtedly points to a significant meaning of the play, that which advances ideas concerning foresight, perception, and blindness to truth; the scene in which the audience is made to see the blinding of Gloucester when the Duke of Cornwall, abetted by his wife Regan, plucks out his eyes is the physical representation on the stage of this imagery: we look in horror at the fate that attends those who had eyes but were blind. Then there are the other themes which are equally obvious: the foolish stubbornness of aged parents; the ingratitude and cruelty of children; man as a naked, forsaken creature in a hostile world; the obligation to endure suffering of unbearable extremity; the treachery and barbarity of humans to their fellows. Then there are the large, and not so obvious, symbolic patterns: for example, Edgar dies a metaphorical death for the sins of others and, resurrected, becomes the bringer of salvation; or the ritual sacrifice of the young daughter before peace and fruitfulness can be restored to the land; or the body's trials on the journey towards spiritual purity. But buried in the opening scene are two other ideas that suggest there are meanings in *King Lear* which have yet to be observed. The first is stated in the brief dialogue between Gloucester and Kent that takes place before Lear enters. It is a reference to Edmund, the bastard, of whom Gloucester says, 'His breeding, sir, hath been at my charge': the father jokes about the 'good sport' that went into his procreation, but what the dialogue establishes is the idea of his illegitimacy: the first of the five children in the play to be seen by the audience is a bastard (and in fact, some texts of the play print his name before his speeches not as EDMUND but as BASTARD). Procreation is associated with blind, playful lust; the consequence of the sporting act is not dignified by 'birth', for it is merely 'breeding' that is occasioned. Once this derogatorily expressed image of breeding new life, as opposed to the more pleasing notion of having children, has been established, Lear then makes his proclamation – *Know that we* – in which the idea concerning certainty of knowledge is suggested.

The idea of worldly property is stressed by Lear. All audiences remember the terrifying moment when he says, 'Tell me, my daughters' and in their memory recall the succeeding words to be, 'Which of you shall we say doth love us most', and indeed the majority of the productions one has seen have presented the speech precisely thus; but the text has something else in it:

> Tell me, my daughters
> (Since now we will divest us both of rule,
> Interest of territory, cares of state),
> Which of you shall we say doth love us most,

most performances eliminate the parenthetical aside, possibly because it reduces the emotional impact of the famous utterance or perhaps because the statement appears to be redundant after Lear's previous lines or that it spoils the neatness of the delivery or diminishes its rhythmic power; the words, however, are important, and the precise idea that they impart has not in fact been implied by the earlier

> and 'tis our fast intent
> To shake all cares and business from our age,
> Conferring them on younger strengths while we
> Unburdened crawl toward death.

The parenthetical remark is a reference to the kingdom, not to responsibility, as these earlier lines are, and it is a necessary addition if the idea of worldly property is to be emphasised – implying a certain knowledge of what it is that is being given up – and the theme created of a man releasing himself from physical attachments and making himself available for a spiritual trial. And nor does the complete statement end with the line, 'Which of you shall we say doth love us most', but continues:

> That we our largest bounty may extend
> Where nature doth with merit challenge.

Lear is giving up being the king and is disposing of his legal claim to possessing the kingdom, but in doing so he gives no clue whether he is being solemnly earnest or merely amusing himself by demanding of his daughters that they fill his ears with a stilted formula of flattery. The fact that he has already divided the kingdom into three and shows the eldest daughter, Goneril, who speaks first, which part is to be hers, and then to the second, Regan, after she has spoken, what she is to receive, pointing after each answer to the map which is there for all to see, indicates that the challenge is not a serious one; if it were, then the three contestants would not be told which part was to be hers until after all three had answered and each answer had been duly weighed by the king for what it merited. But whatever had been Lear's intention – whether he had in mind a real contest or merely a game that mimed kingly power and was played for the didactic purpose of showing what playthings monarchs make of their subjects for the simple reason that it is their whim to do so – his plan is upset by his youngest daughter refusing to play.

The question that, to my knowledge, has never been satisfactorily answered is: why does Cordelia not come up with some glib clichés about love as her sisters do? Why, seeing that her father is so surprised to hear her answer, 'Nothing, my lord', that he can only uncomprehendingly repeat, 'Nothing', and then after he has recovered himself and gives her another chance by asking her to 'Speak again', why does she persist in saying only that which she must know is going to annoy him? Lear as yet is quite patient and he gives Cordelia a third chance when he tells her to 'Mend your speech a little', a statement that is not so much a reprimand as a plea that she, *please*, try once more, for he adds, 'Lest you may mar your fortunes', which seems to suggest that he is eager to settle her fortune and is prepared to forgive in her what might appear to be a passing petulance. Surely, she can hear his hint, but instead of co-operating she makes matters worse by appearing to teach her father a lesson in the love a woman must give her husband, and it is *that* which makes Lear lose his patience and provokes him to disinherit her.

My answer to the question about Cordelia's behaviour is that she has been waiting for an opportunity to alienate her father, that she has acted with deliberate foresight and that she has done so *in order that she may be disinherited by her father*. The misfortune that she seems to bring upon herself may in fact be a state that she has earnestly wanted to achieve, and if so, then her performance of the good little girl who cannot make herself utter obvious untruths like her sisters so glibly do has been a cunning piece of play-acting.

My evidence for Cordelia's premeditated design to provoke her father to disinherit her is based upon the hypothesis that of the two suitors who have come to court her, she has fallen in love with the first, the King of France, and is consequently desperate to prevent the perilous event, which could easily transpire, of some chance determining her father to give her away in marriage to the second suitor, the Duke of Burgundy. Watching out for her own interest, she could also have observed signs that her father has been more inclined to accept Burgundy. She must know that the critical moment has come when hearing her father proclaim the division of the kingdom in three parts, followed by his announcement to his two sons-in-law, Cornwall and Albany, that

> We have this hour a constant will to publish
> Our daughters' several dowers,

she then hears her father refer to her own particular situation:

> The princes, France and Burgundy,
> Great rivals in our youngest daughter's love,
> Long in our court have made their amorous sojourn,
> And here are to be answered.

The time has come for Cordelia's husband to be chosen, and Lear seems about to do so in consultation with his present sons-in-law and the other assembled nobles, or, without wishing to consult, he might be about to announce his decision; whatever he might be about to do, one thing is certainly not being done and that is a private consultation with Cordelia to discover if she has a preference. It has to be, for Cordelia, a terrifying moment.

Long in our court have made their amorous sojourn. How long has been that *long*? At least some weeks, perhaps; possibly some months. And it has been an *amorous* sojourn. Perhaps the suitors have been given the opportunity each to share a private moment with Cordelia. Certainly, there has been time for looks to be exchanged, for a secret preference to be formed. Cordelia is very young (Lear calls her, 'So young, and so untender'). She is at that age when a girl is filled with dreams of love, fixes upon the image of a lover in order to indulge her fantasies and is terrified by potential obstacles that in reality might prevent her attaining the object of her dreams. It has to be inconceivable that Cordelia is exempt from this universal human law; it certainly cannot be, since it is against human nature, that day after day she had looked upon the two men, one of whom is destined to be her husband, and not begun to feel some partial and discriminatory emotion that makes her harbour a secret preference.

The suitors have been at the court long enough for their minds and their characters to be known. The text of the play does not show us any of their behaviour during their long amorous sojourn; however, we do see France and Burgundy respond to Lear's dismissive offer after he has disinherited Cordelia. 'Sir, there she stands', he tells Burgundy, as though she were some broken-down kitchen appliance that had been thrown out of the house and a passer-by were being invited to take it for what it was worth. From the remarks and answers made by France and Burgundy to Lear's contemptuous offer surely one can arrive at a perfectly credible estimation of the character of the two suitors.

Burgundy clearly is more interested in property than he is in love. His first statement is:

> Most royal Majesty,
> I crave no more than hath your Highness offered,
> Nor will you tender less.

When Lear tells him there is nothing but the mere person of Cordelia to be had, Burgundy is so shocked as to be dumbfounded, and says, 'I know no answer.' Lear then puts the question to him bluntly: will Burgundy, now that the only dowry Cordelia has is her father's curse, 'Take her, or leave her?' And Burgundy answers:

> Pardon me, royal sir.
> Election makes not up on such conditions.

The terms Lear is proposing are not the ones on which he can choose. It should be noted that in all these answers, Burgundy makes no reference at all to the actual living person, a beautiful young girl, who is standing in front of him. Only after France appears to be claiming her and Burgundy sees the last hope collapsing of obtaining the property he has coveted, does he make a vague reference to her person, but again the more important words from his mouth concern the prefatory line about property before he can bring himself to mention the name Cordelia:

> Royal King,
> Give but that portion which yourself proposed,
> And here I take Cordelia by the hand.

And when Lear gives him absolute refusal, Burgundy's final words are pathetically tame. He says to Cordelia:

> I am sorry then you have so lost a father
> That you must lose a husband.

Father, husband; but not *daughter, wife*: Burgundy seems incapable of seeing the living woman; his references to her are in terms of male ownership. If this has been the language of his courtship – and after what we hear him say in this scene, it is hard to imagine that he had played the romantic lover during the long amorous sojourn – and if his mind has been so obsessively concerned with property as he demonstrates here, then it is not fanciful to imagine that Cordelia is repelled by him, that she has acquired a perfect hatred for the idea of being married to a man who pays her not the slightest attention, especially when the other suitor appears full of admiration for her person. Her response to Burgundy's statement that she 'must lose a husband' should be noted:

> Peace be with Burgundy.
> Since that respects of fortune are his love,
> I shall not be his wife.

She understands well his passion for fortune and indifference to herself; by referring to him in the third person, she is not only addressing him but also making a general declaration of his character for all to hear, and that final 'I shall not be his wife', which looks like a regretful conclusion resulting from Burgundy's preference for property, can in fact be uttered with inward triumph if the conclusion is seen instead as a happy resolution of her problem. Regret at lost opportunity would have been implied had she said, 'I cannot be his wife', but her *shall not* has a defiant ring about it. There could even be a touch of scorn in that 'I shall not be his wife', for she can afford to be bold with Burgundy now that she is free of him; it is appropriate to observe that by contrast she speaks not a word to France who addresses her directly, heaps high praise upon her, and instantly makes her his queen: she accepts him silently, like one who finding a looked-for treasure in the presence of others must temporarily pretend to have found nothing and must maintain a disappointed face.

Compared to Burgundy's language, France's answers and comments to Lear are full of references to Cordelia; and very warm, ardent, and solicitous references they are too. Where Burgundy's first words had been 'Most royal Majesty, / I crave', France's first statement begins, 'This is most strange, / That she'. Burgundy thinks only of himself, France puts Cordelia before himself: his speeches show him to be someone who has a deep concern for her. It is he who talks of love, giving Burgundy a little lecture:

> Love's not love
> When it is mingled with regards, that stands
> Aloof from th' entire point.

To which he adds a glorious compliment to the young lady: 'She is herself a dowry'. When Burgundy refuses to accept her, France then addresses her thus:

> Fairest Cordelia, that art most rich being poor,
> Most choice forsaken, and most loved despised,
> Thee and thy virtues here I seize upon.

Where Burgundy would *take* Cordelia 'by the hand' as if he were doing her a favour, France, like one whose great good fortune has been to receive a rare gift, would *seize* all of her. Is this not the language of the ardent lover? Therefore, is there not a hint behind these words that – whether through looks, or words, or secret meeting – there is already an understanding between France and Cordelia? He says to Lear:

> Thy dow'rless daughter, King, thrown to my chance,
> Is queen of us, of ours, and our fair France.

It is nobly spoken, and the person upon whom these words must make the strongest impression is Cordelia. The plainness of 'dow'rless' matched with the magnificence of 'queen of us' is spoken in a triumphant voice; and the ironical force with which *King* is isolated in these lines suggests that the king has been outmanœuvred, a hint perhaps that what appears to be a game of chance has in fact been a skillful piece of manipulation. Then he has a parting shot at Burgundy:

> Not all the dukes of wat'rish Burgundy
> Can buy this unprized precious maid of me.

He himself is carrying off the prize, like one who has outwitted his adversary. There is one other moment in this part of the scene which should be noted. Lear says to Cordelia:

> Better thou
> Hadst not been born than not t' have pleased me better.

It is a devastating remark to make to one's offspring. Cordelia does not respond. Perhaps she is so hurt by the cruel words that she is speechless, or too overcome by emotion to speak. It is France who responds. Perhaps he sees Cordelia suddenly overtaken by despair and says words which might comfort her; or perhaps he quickly steps in with a response to prevent her collapsing before her father's anger, but the important point is that it is France who speaks and that what he says is an attempt to diminish the damaging effect upon Cordelia of her father's cruel words and is at the same time an expression of tenderness towards her:

Is it but this? A tardiness in nature
Which often leaves the history unspoke
That it intends to do.

My suggestion, then, is that there has been a prior understanding between Cordelia and France and that in her determination not to be trapped into a marriage with Burgundy she is prepared to exploit any situation that might present itself, especially if the moment that frees her from Burgundy can also be seized by France to make her his bride. It is clear from the language in which Lear talks about her and addresses her – for example, 'Now, our joy' – that Cordelia knows that she is her father's favourite and therefore she can expect to have her way with him; and from the fact that although he has given away two-thirds of his kingdom to the elder sisters after they have dutifully testified to their love for him, she still has reserved for her, as he himself declares, 'A third more opulent', it would follow that he absolutely dotes upon her and therefore it would not be unreasonable for her to be confident that she can manipulate his emotions to have what she wants. When France first speaks, he asks Lear what could Cordelia have done that has led him 'to dismantle / So many folds of favour'; in her final speech before she leaves, Cordelia tells her sisters that 'Time shall unfold what plighted cunning hides': Goneril and Regan have not been so cunning as she herself, for their parroted flattery has been transparent; and it is perhaps not accidental that Cordelia's choice of metaphor should be an echo of what she has a few minutes earlier heard from the man who has now made her his queen.

Also, observe this: after her eldest sister, Goneril, has answered the father's question about how much she loves him, concluding with, 'Beyond all manner of so much I love you', Cordelia turns aside and says to herself, 'What shall Cordelia speak? Love, and be silent'. One has always assumed that what she means by the second sentence is, 'Let me continue to love my father and remain silent'. The context seems to suggest that. But supposing my hypothesis is not incorrect and she has suddenly realised that the moment has come when she must provoke her father to cause the very circumstance which will make her worthless to Burgundy, then her first reaction has to be one of a loss of nerve and the inability of the tongue to speak what it might often have rehearsed: if this scenario were true, then the love she refers to is not the one she feels for her father but for France: 'Love, and be silent' is the phrase of the desperate young girl who cannot speak of her real emotion. The next time she speaks is after her second sister, Regan, has glibly enunciated her string of clichés of how much she loves her father. Now Cordelia says in an aside:

> Then poor Cordelia;
> And yet not so, since I am sure my love's
> More ponderous than my tongue.

Here, again, the context seems to suggest that she must be referring to her love for her father; but – and this, in spite of all appearances, cannot be denied – there is no certainty that she might not be referring to a love about which she finds it impossible to talk, for it has been her secret. So that when her father, having disposed of the elder sisters, turns to her and dangles before her the 'more opulent' third of the kingdom, all she can come up with is 'Nothing, my lord', so overcome she must be in that moment by her nerves, her emotions, and her terror that one false step and she will be married off to Burgundy. So, Lear asks her to speak again, and she manages a longer statement which, however, only serves to confuse the old father, who responds, 'How, how, Cordelia?' It is then, on being given this third chance to speak clearly so that she might not lose her fortune, that she speaks her little lesson to her father:

> Good my lord,
> You have begot me, bred me, loved me. I

> Return those duties back as are right fit,
> Obey you, love you, and most honour
> you.

She goes on, in the six lines that follow, to make the pointed remark that as a wife she will have to give half her love to her husband. It is a neat little speech. The major part of this speech alludes to a woman's love for her husband, and sounds as if it is a subject uppermost in her mind. In short, her references to love when we think the love in question is for the father are more often to the love for the man she hopes will be her husband.

But, of course, the violent nature of Lear's response is a great shock to her. She might have expected the kind of outrage and anger sufficient to provoke from her father that momentary suspension of her rights to a dowry which would have been sufficient to gain her end of eliminating Burgundy from the contest for her hand; but the finality of Lear's rejection of her must indeed have caused despair and grief so great as to make her repent. In Act I, scene i, when she alienates her father, she is as much looking out for herself as are her sisters; what matters it if she must lose her third of Britain when she can be Queen of France? But the unexpected happens.

If she has manipulated her own rejection by her father and given away her inheritance for the sake of France, the severity of her father's rejection must begin to pain her when news reaches her of her sisters' cruelty to the father. It must surely occur to her that had she not lost her inheritance then there would have been a place where the outcast father would have been welcome. And if the father's rejection and the loss of her land, and the father's homelessness, are seen by her as a consequence of her own actions, then her guilt must be intense. She repents and martyrs herself to her father's love. It is not only her love that brings her back to him; it is also her own pressing need for expiation.

When Lear rejects her, his first words contain a reference

to the ideas concerning knowledge and property that he had expressed in his first speech:

> Let it be so, thy truth then be thy dower!

Let it be so can be seen as an assertion made in opposition to the earlier *Know that we*: where in the first speech Lear wished the court and his sons-in-law to know that he himself held the material world in such exclusive possession that the division of the kingdom was the exercise only of his own will, an act both authoritative and generous; he himself was the complete commander of reality – even of the future, believing that his benevolent foresight would prevent 'future strife'. He had not expected the youngest daughter's refusal to accept his neat re-arrangement of reality and therefore the phrase *Let it be so* is charged first with his outrage that Cordelia has the presumption that she has a free will and secondly with a despairing resignation that he himself does not possess a supreme control over reality; the remark that follows, 'thy truth then be thy dower', is bitterly ironical: where the king had offered property – material wealth – Cordelia is going to have to be content with an abstraction – spiritual wealth; a third of the kingdom is definitely there upon the map before them, which is to say, the phenomenological world is present to human perception, but Lear is the first no longer to see it, for he himself invites his sons-in-law to 'digest the third', so that unwittingly he himself presides over the dissolution of a reality of which he had possessed such certain knowledge when he had begun with *Know that we*; the thing is no longer there, it is eaten up, and it is ironical that this thing is 'truth'. In dismissing Cordelia, Lear hits upon an image expressive of his terrible wrath: he would prefer the company of a savage who eats his own children to his own 'sometime daughter'.

That *sometime daughter* is more than the spontaneous cruelty of an angry parent. Lear is stripping Cordelia of her legitimacy, making her a bastard who, having no claim to her father's property, is cast into permanent exile from his land even before she physically removes herself from it. Her inheritance is thrown at Cornwall and Albany to be quickly consumed, and Lear's use of the word 'digest' seems to bear a memory of the cannibalistic image spoken a moment earlier, so that there is a buried association of Lear having become the savage eating his own child. Truth is to be Cordelia's dowry, pride her husband; after bestowing materially worthless abstractions upon the 'sometime daughter', Lear does not observe that he is disinheriting himself in precisely the same manner when he gives away the wealth of his kingdom, reserving for himself only the *name* of king, only, that is, an idea without substance. In a final symbolic representation of parting with his kingdom, he gives away his crown, saying to the sons-in-law, 'This coronet part between you'. He has now divested himself of all worldly property.

When Kent tries to make him see the folly of his action in disinheriting Cordelia and in abandoning his own kingly authority, Lear first shouts at him, 'Out of my sight!', and then banishes him – that is, exiles him from the physical realm as unknowingly he has himself. It is interesting to note that when Kent begins to make his appeal with a string of conventional epithets, 'Royal Lear . . . my great patron . . .', Lear cuts him short with, 'The bow is bent and drawn; make from the shaft', the literal meaning of which image is obvious enough. What is not so obvious is that Lear, who has just separated himself from the physical realm, is here metaphorically offering a self-sacrifice. Having divested himself of worldly property, he is here making a symbolic renunciation of the body by himself inviting the arrow his imagination sees is aimed at him.

Lear is like one who has resolved to prepare for a spiritual quest and must observe the prescribed rules: first he must give away his worldly possessions and then he must submit his body to that extreme punishment which is a form of a living death. The living death is to be willingly accepted because it seems a necessary act of atonement for past error: the body's final journey is to be through pain, deprivation and humiliation – afflictions that shoot arrows into the flesh. Once this living death has been experienced, the real death that must follow is not only not to be feared but is to be welcomed either as a release or a renewal. In the suffering that Lear brings upon himself are to be seen mythological images of universal potency.

In the closing lines of Act I, scene i, Goneril and Regan confer briefly to resolve upon a common plan, and the latter observes of Lear that 'he hath ever but slenderly known himself', a remark that rounds off the scene with a neat irony by echoing the *Know that we* of Lear's opening speech which is now perceived as indicating the presumptuous assurance of a man deficient in self-knowledge; also, a man who knows himself 'but slenderly' cannot rationally understand the deeper significance of the events in which he becomes involved but will receive an intuitive knowledge of it when, having lost physical reality, he comes to lose his mind.

*

Act I, scene ii: Enter Edmund, and his first words are, 'Thou, Nature, art my goddess'. The nature he refers to is more the art of trickery in a rational world of malicious cause and evil effect than that Nature which is a divine intelligence ruling the universe. Presently, in Act I, scene iv, Lear will be heard to use similar words, 'Hear, Nature, hear; dear goddess, hear', when he appeals to the divinity, calling for sterility to afflict his eldest daughter who has deeply offended him. The Bastard's reference to Nature is cynical and contemptuous; when his father Gloucester attributes recent disasters to 'eclipses in the sun and moon', Edmund ridicules such explanations, dismisses the concept of planetary influence over human conduct, and maintains the pre-eminence of free will by which humans choose and shape their own destiny. He concludes: 'I should have been that I am, had the maidenliest star in the firmament twinkled on my bastardising'. Where Gloucester talks of the 'bias of nature', Edmund insists upon the power of the human will to govern events. Succeeding in his immediate plan to make his father believe that his legitimate son Edgar is plotting parricide while suggesting to Edgar that his enraged father intends serious injury upon his person, Edmund proves to himself that effects are caused by people, not the stars; at the end of Act I, scene ii, when he has manipulated his 'credulous father' and 'noble' brother to follow his will, he refers to Edgar's gentle 'nature', echoing the Nature of his opening speech but now reducing the concept to an easily exploitable quality; and it is with a boastful self-assurance that he concludes:

> Let me, if not by birth, have lands by wit;
> All with me's meet that I can fashion fit.

While Act I, scene ii sets a sub-plot in motion, it also serves to establish the abstract concepts of Nature and identity that are of a wider consequence in the play. Edmund's conviction about his own being will be tested in the final scene of the play when, soon after Regan creates him her 'lord and master', giving him a grander identity than the title of the Earl of Gloucester which he had earlier usurped, he is challenged by the unidentified Edgar who when asked to identify himself answers, 'Know my name is lost', and in the combat that follows, kills Edmund, leaving nothing of the names he had acquired by exercising his manipulative nature.

The question of identity is alluded to from beginning to end, from Kent's asking Gloucester in Act I, scene i of Edmund, 'Is not this your son, my lord?' to Lear's recognising Kent for who he is in the final minutes of the play when we hear from Kent the very simple words, 'I am the very man'. In Act I, scene i, when Lear has disinherited Cordelia, he offers her to Burgundy with the words, 'Sir, there she stands'. He points to her 'little seeming substance' and concludes, 'She's there, and she is yours'. Not only has she been stripped of her fortune; Lear's language strips her down to her plain being. The exiled Kent disguises himself so that he can continue to serve the king; 'I razed my likeness', he says in Act I, scene iv, just before Lear enters and asks, 'How now, what art thou?' When Kent applies, 'A man, sir', the answer is rejected as insufficient, and after Kent has given a longer description of himself, Lear repeats, possibly with greater emphasis, 'What art thou?' In the same scene, when Lear thinks himself insulted by Oswald, he asks him, 'Who am I, sir?' Later in Act I, scene iv, when he has become more angry, Lear demands,

> Does any here know me? This is not Lear.
> Does Lear walk thus? speak thus? Where are his eyes?
> . . . Who is it that can tell me who I am?

'Lear's shadow', mutters the Fool in a seemingly automatic response that sounds philosophically cruel; the Fool's remark, however, anticipates a more conclusively expressed answer to the question of human identity that comes at the end of *Macbeth* where living form is projected as nothing but 'a walking shadow'. And then, of course, there is the famous moment in Act III, scene iv when Lear comes upon the unclothed Edgar and asks, 'Is man no more than this?' and then declares, 'Thou art the thing itself', requiring no definition; observing that truth, however, Lear fails to recognise the implied truth of his own failure to perceive that he himself had, when presenting Cordelia to Burgundy, reduced her to 'the thing itself' but at that time equated her bare, disinherited being with her ceasing to exist.

Goneril strips Lear of his idea of himself. When Lear asks, 'Who is it that can tell me who I am?' his question is, of course, a rhetorical one, and except for the Fool who is free to make comments which no one is obliged to take seriously – and, therefore, he is a privileged presence whose insights are those of a seer – no one is expected to attempt an answer, for Lear's question draws attention to his presumed, and long-established, majesty, to his generally known identity as King of Britain. He sees upon his person 'marks of sovereignty / Knowledge, and reason', which everyone present except Goneril must believe to be a just claim. But she coldly informs him that he is an old man and scolds him for keeping a 'disordered rabble' about him, making her house seem 'like a tavern or a brothel'. She demands he reduce the number of his followers. Lear is so enraged by what he believes to be her ingratitude that he pronounces a chilling curse upon her:

> Hear, Nature, hear; dear goddess, hear:
> Suspend thy purpose if thou didst intend
> To make this creature fruitful.
> Into her womb convey sterility,
> Dry up in her the organs of increase,
> And from her derogate body never spring
> A babe to honour her.

It is the father's ultimate curse upon his own child, that she remain childless. In the earlier tragedies, Hamlet expresses a horror of having been born and does not wish his mother to repeat the act that had caused his own birth; Othello has scarcely consummated his marriage when he kills his bride; in the final tragedy, Macbeth is responsible for the murder of children and his wife uses the image of plucking away a nursing baby from her breast and dashing its brains out. In each of the four plays sexuality and procreation constitute significant imagery if not also a central theme. Implied in this imagery is an implacable criticism, if not rejection, of birth. *King Lear* begins with a dialogue about procreation, with remarks about the 'good sport' that went into the making of the bastard. When Lear pronounces his curse upon Goneril, it is an expression of rage against legitimate offspring; the curse is essentially against himself, for it calls for a cessation of his own line; but when in Act II, scene iv he receives a more cruel rejection from his second daughter Regan, he calls his daughters 'unnatural hags', thus putting them into a category worse than that of bastard, creatures that he himself could not have fathered since they are unnatural: the curse cuts off his future heirs and thus it is he himself who is truly sterile, and of the living proof of his fertility, one daughter has been disowned and the other two branded unnatural so that he absolves himself from the association of guilt attending their birth. Also, if the 'unnatural hags' are indeed his own acknowledged progeny, then children are seen to be worse than bastards engendered by sport: they are deformities disowned by nature.

Cursing Goneril, Lear parts from her with the defiant words:

> Thou shalt find
> That I'll resume the shape which thou dost think
> I have cast off for ever.

He is going to his second daughter and believes that she will unquestioningly honour his wishes: Regan will, so to speak, restore the rights that Goneril has suspended and Lear will resume his former shape. But Regan will go one further; what Goneril has suspended, Regan will abolish, and where Lear expects to be welcomed the door is to be shut against him. Dispossessed of his land, his crown, and his children, Lear will find himself amidst the great chaos of elemental nature: and there, he indeed will 'resume the shape' which not Goneril but he himself had thought he had 'cast off for ever', the shape that he had of 'the thing itself', the bare being that belongs to no physical realm and has no material attachments: it is the being of a man with no past and no future, a consciousness cast out of the dimension of time, and of that shape, too, which is prior to consciousness, the shape of not having been born which is resumed at death.

Just as Lear loses the physical realm, Edmund gains it. In words that he invents for his brother, Edmund calls himself the 'unpossessing bastard': the phrase is used in Act II, scene i, soon after Act I has concluded by casting Lear out of his first daughter's house, altering his condition from the King of Britain to a homeless old man. Edmund has begun by having no possessions, being born a bastard; what he acquires is had by cunning and deceit: he comes to possess land, title and the jealous love of Lear's two elder daughters by becoming a destructive agent against his own family. He manipulates his father to disinherit the legitimate heir, and advances rapidly to gain power in Lear's former kingdom by betraying his own father to Regan. Regan's husband, Cornwall, is mortally wounded when he is in the act of blinding Edmund's father, an event that first leads to Edmund assuming his father's title, the Earl of Gloucester, and then, with Cornwall dead, to Regan's subsequently proclaiming him her 'lord and master'. When she does so, she significantly offers him her 'patrimony', so that Edmund, the 'unpossessing bastard', comes to possess in materially a very full sense all that was Lear's whereas Lear, in losing his kingdom and being deprived by his children of the legitimate claims of parenthood, assumes the condition of the 'unpossessing bastard'. In Lear and Edmund, it is as if the self and the anti-self were locked in a mutually destructive embrace; at the end of the play, Lear dies just after a messenger comes and announces the death of Edmund: the self and the anti-self cancel each other out almost simultaneously. Edgar, the legitimate heir, had been given his name by Lear, the king exercising the prerogative of the father. The living Edmund had stolen his brother's name by stealing his inheritance. When Lear dies, Edgar becomes the king. It is as if Lear had named him again, recreating in him all that he himself had been and repossessing for him the land of which he himself had become unpossessed. 'The wheel has come full circle', states Edmund after he has been mortally wounded by the mysterious knight who, announcing 'my name is lost', challenges Edmund and then, having felled him, announces, 'My name is Edgar and thy father's son'. He reclaims his name, his honour, his property; he inherits the material realm and finally his is the kingdom.

*

The banished Kent disguises himself in order to continue to serve Lear, and in his disguise he is the unknown seer who sees through the disguises of others. 'I know thee not', Goneril's steward Oswald tells him. 'Fellow, I know thee', replies Kent. 'What does thou know me for?' demands Oswald and receives a long mouthful of abuse in answer: he is called a remarkably lengthy list of names, beginning with a 'knave' and going on to 'coward' and 'pander'; the most graphic term of abuse is held to the end: Kent calls Oswald 'the son and heir of a mongrel bitch'.

Kent can think of nothing worse to call Oswald. It will be remembered that in the opening scene of the play it was to Kent that Gloucester had said of his bastard son, 'His breeding, sir, hath been at my charge', in which speech the idea had been established of procreation as a mindless act. Now Kent gives an imagistic emphasis to that idea and by associating procreation with the activity of a mongrel bitch who when on heat is mounted by every dog in the neighbourhood who can sniff her out the idea suggested by Kent is that of children being bred in the manner of unwanted puppies.

When Cornwall demands why he is so angry, Kent heaps another string of epithets upon Oswald:

> Such smiling rogues as these
> Like rats oft bite the holy cords atwain
> Which are too intrinse t' unloose;

Kent presents here the implied ideal of a sacred bond in some eternally preserved moral order in which duty and virtue prevail; but the reality he sees about him has none of that intrinsic goodness and therefore his sensibility, outraged by the collapse of that just order, can express its overwhelming disappointment only in a language of vile abuse. Once again the image of dogs comes to his mind, and he refers to Oswald's type of lackey as

> With every gale and vary of their masters,
> Knowing naught, like dogs, but following.

When Cornwall decides to punish Kent by putting him in the stocks and Regan says that he must remain there all night, Kent says:

> Why, madam, if I were your father's dog,
> You should not use me so.

Kent falls asleep in the stocks, and in the quickly succeeding scene (Act II, scene iii), Edgar appears and talks about his own condition as that of a hunted animal. The purpose of his soliloquy is to show the necessity for his conversion from Edgar to poor Tom, from the recognisable social being to 'the thing itself'. He has decided, he says,

> To take the basest and most poorest shape
> That ever penury, in contempt of man,
> Brought near to beast:

The shape that he proceeds to take is not unlike that of 'the son and heir of a mongrel bitch'.

In the following scene, Lear comes upon the punished Kent. The Fool jokes about Kent's condition in the stocks: remarking upon the manner in which various animals are restrained, including in his list dogs who are tied by the neck and men by the legs, the Fool concludes: 'When a man's over-lusty at legs, then he wears wooden nether-stocks'. The image upon the stage is that of the restrained Kent, no different from the condition of a dog who, being 'over-lusty', must be prevented from pursuing some mongrel bitch. When Regan appears before her father and says, 'I am glad to see your Highness', Lear responds:

> If thou shouldst not be glad
> I would divorce me from thy mother's tomb,
> Sepulchring an adultress.

The child lacking in duty cannot be one's natural offspring and the wife who gave her birth must have strayed bitch-like from the marriage bed when she conceived.

Lear proceeds to complain to Regan about Goneril's 'Sharp-toothed unkindness', behaving towards the father as a vulture and as a serpent. But Regan suggests that her elder sister's actions have been perfectly correct and says that Lear ought to return to Goneril and apologise to her: it is he who, being old, is behaving unnaturally. The memory of the eldest daughter's rejection makes Lear explode with imprecations and curses. It is not enough that 'All the stored vengeance of heaven' should fall upon Goneril's ungrateful head, but Lear demands a particular and detailed mutilation of Goneril's body: she must be afflicted in 'her young bones' 'with lameness'; lightning must strike 'blinding flames' into her 'scornful eyes'; and her beauty must be disfigured by pock marks. Lear's curses against Goneril are calculated to make her physically so look like an unnatural hag that the world may witness that she could not be his true daughter.

The graphic vileness of his curses also, of course, serves an immediate dramatic purpose. Lear believes he has come to a kinder and a more understanding and accommodating daughter, while the audience knows that she is as serpent-like as her sister; so that when after heaping his curses upon Goneril Lear speaks twelve gentle lines to Regan, praising her 'tender-hefted nature', the irony is keenly felt by the audience which anticipates the severity of Regan's rejection: the more he rails against Goneril and the more softspoken he is in his estimation of Regan the worse his situation will presently become. But before Regan can answer and reveal her true self, Goneril arrives and soon Lear is rendered almost speechless by their combined rejection: he wants to take some terrible revenge against them that he 'will do such things' – but he cannot think of anything ('What they are, yet I know not'), having earlier piled up such an exhaustive list of graphic curses and having added a few new vile terms on seeing Goneril whom he calls a 'boil', a 'plague-sore' and an 'embossèd carbuncle' in his own 'corrupted blood'. Unable to think of any more particular curses, he can do little more than exclaim, 'No, you unnatural hags!', and leave to enter the storm and tempest which have begun to rage outside.

The elements have become the 'servile ministers' of the 'pernicious daughters' and are heaping the outrage of extreme inclemency upon Lear who now believes himself 'A poor, infirm, weak, and despised old man'. At first, coming out into the storm, he is all defiance in a language of unmatched monosyllabic magnificence: 'Blow, winds, and crack your cheeks. Rage, blow'. It is almost as if he took the howling rage of nature and howled right back at it, caught the thunder in his throat and made of it hard and rolling words with which to strike back:

> And thou, all-shaking thunder,
> Strike flat the thick rotundity o' th' world,
> Crack nature's moulds, all germains spill at once,
> That makes ingrateful man.

He invites the storm to acquire a more destructive ferocity. What good is reality when he must lose the world? Let the world be levelled, devastated. Let all forms of things be smashed into dust. Let the semen of the world be poured into some black hole. The Fool's intercession that 'Here's a night pities neither wise men nor fools', suggesting that nature is deaf and blind and serves no man, does not stop Lear who shouts at the sky:

> Rumble thy bellyful. Spit, fire. Spout, rain.

The power of the storm to inflict pain upon him associates it with his two daughters in Lear's mind, for the raging elements have joined with Goneril and Regan to wage 'high-engendered battles' against his 'old and white' head. His rage is exhausted before the storm's, a calm comes over him, and this is the moment of transformation, when he goes mad; he is no longer the Lear whose kingdom was a piece of real estate neatly delineated upon a map and contained 'shadowy forests' and 'champaigns riched', his were fertile lands to bestow upon children none of whom had yet drawn the curse of sterility; now Lear is where Kent finds him, under the 'wrathful skies' which are lit up by 'sheets of fire' and filled with 'horrid thunder' and 'groans of roaring wind and rain', and now, going mad, Lear has a moment of sublime intuition that his ranting is futile:

> No, I will be the pattern of all patience;
> I will say nothing.

In the middle of the raging storm he has found the still centre in which recognition comes that his real affliction is internal:

> The tempest in my mind
> Doth from my senses take all feeling else
> Save what beats there.

And the storm continuing with unabated ferocity, Lear comes upon the transformed Edgar and first is so amazed to see the reduction of man to the condition of a naked wretch that he asks, 'Is man no more than this?' and soon concluding that 'Thou art the thing itself' realises that he himself can expect to be no more.

*

On receiving news from Kent of her father's homeless and deranged condition, Cordelia returns to Britain and in her first speech commands her soldiers to search the countryside for Lear 'And bring him to our eye'.

The eye imagery in *King Lear*, with its easily comprehended attendant ideas pertaining to perception and vision, has been much made of, but it is so obviously present throughout the play that one would need to be an exceptionally dormant playgoer not to notice it. The emphasis of

Lear's 'Out of my sight!' to Kent in Act I, scene i, when Kent has attempted to intercede on behalf of Cordelia, followed by Kent's 'See better, Lear, and let me still remain / The true blank of thine eye' establishes the imagistic pattern early in the play and there is not a major character in it who does not exploit some related image. 'Let's see', says Gloucester to Edmund in Act I, scene ii, falling blindly into the bastard's trap, 'Come, if it be nothing, I shall not need spectacles'. In his overwhelming emotion when he is rejected by Goneril in Act I, scene iv, Lear begs his own 'Old fond eyes' not to weep and threatens to pluck them out if they do; in the same scene, Albany remarks to his wife, 'How well your eyes may pierce I cannot tell'. There are several more references to eyes before Act III, scene vii, in which Gloucester is blinded, first one eye, and then the other, plucked out in a moment of chilling horror by Cornwall who says, 'Lest it see more, prevent. Out, vile jelly'. And even in that moment the excessive exploitation of the imagery continues for Cornwall being wounded by a servant even as he is blinding Gloucester, Regan says to him, 'How is't, my lord? How look you?' And several more references follow in the rest of the play. In the scene in which Goneril and Albany quarrel (Act IV, scene ii), she accuses him of not having 'in thy brows an eye discerning / Thine honour from thy suffering' and he responds, 'See thyself, devil'. And, of course, much irony and emotion are extracted from images of seeing whenever the blind Gloucester is present, the most touching scene being when Edgar pretends he is describing a frightful fall from a hilltop (Act IV, scene vi): 'How fearful / And dizzy 'tis to cast one's eyes so low!' and concludes

> I'll look no more,
> Lest my brain turn, and the deficient sight
> Topple down headlong.

In the same scene, Lear says to Gloucester, 'If thou wilt weep my fortunes, take my eyes'. Lear's final words before he dies are, 'Look there, look there,' and indeed, the references continue to the very last line of the play in which Edgar says that the young 'Shall never see so much'.

Only a very naïve spectator or reader will miss this imagistic pattern which seems to have been so woven by an over-eager hand as to make some of the associated irony appear forced. The point about foresight, or lack of it, has long been made before Cordelia returns from France and asks for her father to be brought before her eyes. She concludes the same speech by offering to whoever can help restore her father's sanity all her 'outward worth', a remark of double significance which first emphatically implies that she places no value on property and also suggests that no one can take from her the real thing of value, her inward worth. The notion of her internal strength evokes the conception of her that had been formed in Act I, scene i, as a strong-willed person, thus effecting a perception of continuity and consistency in her character. It is to be noted, too, that when France had taken her for his queen her 'outward worth' then had been nothing and what France had seized had been no more than 'the thing itself' which her father had dismissed as 'that little seeming substance'. Now her 'outward worth' is substantial and yet it is worth nothing because she is prepared to give it all away in exchange for her father's sanity; a mad father cannot see her but as a delusion or as a tormenting fantasy of what hurts his mind most and therefore if her giving away her 'outward worth' were to coincide with the restoration of his sanity then he would see her without the outer unreliable identity, which is to say he would see her as 'the thing itself'.

There are 'blessed secrets' in nature and 'unpublished virtues of the earth' which are symbolically watered by Cordelia's tears so that the herbs that grow may remedy 'the good man's distress'. While she would find from nature the mind-altering drug which could free her father from a delusional perception of reality, Edgar is obliged to re-invent reality in order to produce a delusional representation of it for his blind father who has asked him to take him to a hilltop. Standing on flat ground, he creates a picture of immense height from where fishermen walking on the beach below look like mice and the ocean's 'murmuring surge' cannot be heard. Gloucester leaps to kill himself but merely falls upon the ground in front of him. Edgar, now pretending to be some other who happens to be walking on the beach below where Gloucester has been misled to believe he has fallen, utters to him his amazement that he should have plunged 'So many fathom down' and not been hurt. 'Thy life's a miracle', says Edgar. Poor Gloucester cries, 'But have I fall'n, or no?' Edgar replies:

> From the dread summit of this chalky bourn.
> Look up a-height. The shrill-gorged lark so far
> Cannot be seen or heard. Do but look up.

If only one could 'but look up', an enchanting reality painted by the imagination is to be perceived; the lark may be too far to be seen but it is there at least as a conception of language which implants a more enduring picture in the mind than the bird caught in a fleeting spot of sunlight and then lost in shadow for ever. Edgar's speeches, attempting to create a believable imaginary reality in order to protect and preserve his blind father, are followed in the same scene by what at first appear to be the mad rantings of Lear who now enters, the stage direction states, *'mad, bedecked with weeds'*, and declares 'I am the King himself', sublimely echoing 'Thou art the thing itself'. In his first short speech in which he makes a series of unconnected utterances which are heard as evidence of his having gone mad, he makes the remarkable statement, 'Nature 's above art in that respect' in response to Edgar's pitying 'O thou side-piercing sight!'

There seems no connection between Edgar's words, which essentially comprise a thought within his own mind, and Lear's remark which has the appearance of a deliberate conclusion as if it were an idea arrived at after other hypotheses had been tested and rejected. We have just observed an example of art – Edgar's verbal creation of a high hill with a precipitous fall, which we see as clearly as the blind Gloucester must imagine it – but Lear now informs us that nature cannot be altered. The thing itself remains itself. Though this seems conclusively to suggest that there is an absolute and unalterable substance to reality, Lear's own subsequent speeches undermine his own neat axiom, for his deranged mind creates a fanciful language, seeing before him what is not there – 'There's hell, there's darkness, there is the sulphurous pit' – an imagery as compelling as had been Edgar's about the view from the hilltop. A madman's hallucinations are no less valid as ideas than are the images of a fantastic composition of preposterous facts.

Lear's troubled mind imagines one accused of adultery, and he says:

> Thou shalt not die. Die for adultery? No.
> The wren goes to't, and the small gilded fly
> Does lecher in my sight.

And in the next line he announces as if he proclaimed a decree from the throne: 'Let copulation thrive', and proceeds to list examples of lechery in the animal kingdom, projecting a particularly vile impression of uninhibited and obsessive sexuality which results in mindless breeding. In his madness, he tells the truth about society: the beadle who would lash the whore in fact lusts after her; while the vices of the poor are plainly apprehended, those of the rich are hidden behind 'Robes and furred gowns'; justice pierces the poor but is corrupted by gold when the same crime is committed by the rich; and so on. The dwelling upon uninhibited copulation as a universal phenomenon both in nature and in human society revives the idea suggested by the play's opening scene where Gloucester refers to the sport that went into the breeding of the bastard Edmund.

And like the mad of tradition who unknowingly utter wisdom, so Lear:

> When we are born, we cry that we are come
> To this great stage of fools.

It is at the conclusion of this speech that Cordelia's men find Lear. Edgar, still trying to protect his father, finds himself in danger of having his true identity discovered and feigns a peasant's dialect so that though he uses words to convey ideas his language sounds like a yokel's gibberish. The scene (Act IV, scene vi) had begun with Edgar's invented description with which to delude his father and now, after one more example of an invented language (and this gibberish of Edgar's is an echo too of Lear's apparent nonsense), ends in a magnificent irony with the father wishing he were mad so that his thoughts would not dwell upon his suffering, that in his distracted state he could be so possessed by delusions that his troubles would lose 'The knowledge of themselves'.

Now the drama moves to its most poignant scenes, from Act IV, scene vii, in which Cordelia has begun to nurse her father back to health, to the end. Waking and seeing his youngest daughter, Lear believes he must have died, for he says to her:

> Thou art a soul in bliss; but I am bound
> Upon a wheel of fire, . . .

and doubts that he is among the living, asking 'Where have I been? Where am I?'.

The worst of his mental crisis is over and a serenity seems to descend upon him. The arrogant, worldly Lear of the play's opening scene has become humble, meek, and says of himself, 'I am a very foolish fond old man'; the daughter he had then disowned he now claims as 'my child Cordelia' to which, thrilled at the affirmation of her being, she exclaims, 'And so I am! I am!' Lear touches her tears. 'Yes, faith.' They are wet. She is real. In Act V, scene ii, while the battle rages between the forces of France and of the two sisters led by Edmund and Albany, Cordelia is seen leading Lear by the hand.

The battle echoes the earlier sounds of the violent storm under which the homeless Lear had lost his sanity and fallen into hell. Now he has climbed out of that hell, and not war nor the treachery of men can threaten his serenity as long as he is companioned by the 'soul in bliss'. They are taken prisoners by the victorious Edmund, but Lear is unconcerned. 'We two alone will sing like birds i' th' cage', he says to Cordelia. The material condition of existence has become irrelevant. The divided kingdom that was precisely marked out on the map no longer exists for him. He and Cordelia will 'pray, and sing, and tell old tales' in the bird's cage of their prison, the tiny confining space in which Lear shall be freer than he was as the King of Britain, and in that liberty of the soul they will 'take upon' themselves 'the mystery of things' as if they were 'God's spies'.

All shall be known to him who has been bound to the wheel of fire as his body has endured the suffering that finally releases him from desire. 'I will endure', Lear had said when he had first felt the tempest within his mind (Act III, scene iv); and Edgar, whose suffering also is like that of one nailed to the cross, declares, 'Men must endure' (Act V, scene ii). Both do. Having been saved by an angelic spirit, Lear gains spiritual serenity and, becoming God's spy, has therefore acquired a visionary knack and is no longer the earlier Lear who had been told by Kent to 'See better'. Lear is raised to the divine visionary realm where he needs no kingdom for his body. Edgar's endurance is unaided; no angelic hand takes him up. His is a miraculous resurrection.

But it is life's final delusion that the body will be freed of desire and spiritual serenity be experienced. Human treachery and evil will not permit it. Lear must helplessly carry the sacrificed daughter and stumble howling across the stage. There is no vision, only fact stated in the simplest language: 'She's dead as earth.' There is no release from pain, and Lear who only now was planning to 'sing like birds' is heard to cry, 'Howl, howl, howl!'

Macbeth: The Feverous Earth

'Fair is foul, and foul is fair,' chant in chorus the three witches in the first scene of *Macbeth*. In the second scene, a wounded, bleeding captain appears before King Duncan to report the glorious deeds in battle of the 'brave Macbeth' and employs a striking metaphor of a thunderstorm that follows a bright sunrise to describe how fortune in battle can swing from early advantage to near catastrophe –

> As whence the sun 'gins his reflection
> Shipwracking storms and direful thunders break,

– words that vividly objectify the abstract concept of the fair/foul duality. In the third scene, Macbeth enters with Banquo. His first words in the play, spoken as he comes to the stage, are

> So foul and fair a day I have not seen.

There is nothing in the play to suggest that there is unusual weather over Scotland, and surely there can be nothing new about days when bright sunshine and stormy clouds succeed each other with a conspicuous competitiveness. Because his success in battle has made it an auspicious day for him there could possibly be a special poignancy to this particular day's changing weather that makes Macbeth notice it, but his remark could be a clue to another idea – that unknown to him he has, on this day, a perception of reality which is new to him. The victorious soldier, returning to his sovereign in whose name he has defended the land, for which service he is presently to receive a new title that will increase his worldly honour, this man rooted so firmly in the physically solid world of incontestable facts is suddenly halted in his career and shown something he has not seen before: what seemed certain in reality is not so, for successive events in nature seem contradictory or inconsistent, one with the other, and the very image before him proclaims its opposite. Hardly has Macbeth uttered his first line than he is staring at creatures who appear to be women but who have beards on their faces – a precise simultaneous representation in one objective image of *foul and fair*.

A man of action, Macbeth is hardly the kind of person to be oppressed by doubts concerning reality or even to think there can be any existence other than the solidly materialistic. His thinking admits no abstraction: where a Hamlet reflects on *being*, Macbeth talks of a 'brief candle', and even his 'walking shadow' has a visible presence. To such a man, it is inconceivable that things are anything but what they appear to be. A dagger is a dagger. Ambiguity, duality, otherness – these are empty words. As a military man, he is accustomed to real targets, not windmills, to conquering real territory, not Erewhon. And it is precisely because of his unquestioning belief that reality is a non-negotiable item, a sort of inalienable right of common perception, that when a doubt intrudes into his mind it is not as an intellectual questioning but it comes as subliminal experience that begins to threaten the brain with symptoms of disorder: psychosis, epilepsy, hallucinations. Before long, he will see a dagger where there is none.

The theme of the simultaneous presence of contradictory ideas in one object is continued when the witches inform Banquo that he is 'Lesser than Macbeth, and greater'. His fate is 'Not so happy, yet much happier.' His descendants will be kings, but he will not be one himself. He is the personification of the the idea of *foul and fair*. When later Macbeth will have received confirmation that Banquo has been murdered, he will talk of him in fair terms as 'the grac'd person of our Banquo' and will immediately be confounded by the presence of the foul – the murdered man's ghost at whom he will shout, 'Hence horrible shadow,' anticipating the language of his final despair with reality, adding, 'Unreal mockery hence'.

When at the beginning of the play the witches vanish after making their prophecies, Macbeth remarks, that 'what seemed corporal melted / As breath into the wind'. The weather; the paradoxical, contradictory and unbelievable, but in the end strangely persuasive, language of the witches; and now their sudden vanishing before his eyes, which witness solidity become instantaneously converted to nothing, are all challenging the soldierly man's convictions. It is as if Yeats's 'Solider Aristotle' stared amazedly at Plato's 'ghostly paradigm of things'. Banquo perhaps echoes Macbeth's wonder at the sudden corruption of unquestioned beliefs:

> Were such things here as we do speak about?
> Or have we eaten on the insane root
> That takes the reason prisoner?

Hardly has the thought been expressed that at least some phenomena in the universe must be illusory when evidence comes to confirm their being real: the witches have just vanished, Banquo has just suggested that he and Macbeth could be in the grip of hallucination when Ross and Angus, noblemen of Scotland, come from the king and by announcing to Macbeth his new title of Thane of Cawdor echo what the witches had proclaimed and thus give him proof that the bearded women were not creatures of his fancy but the real deliverers of prophecy. Banquo observes the elation that has begun to possess Macbeth and cautions:

> But 'tis strange:
> And oftentimes, to win us to our harm,
> The instruments of darkness tell us truths,
> Win us with honest trifles, to betray's
> In deepest consequence.

As, indeed, does nature with its infinite capacity for inventing camouflage that gives to some creatures the illusion of a magical protection against harm while encouraging them to stray into that light where the waiting predator is not deceived by what it looks at, and fair turns quickly to foul.

Still elated, Macbeth believes the witches were instruments not of darkness but of prophecy. He has no doubt and asserts categorically:

> Two truths are told,
> As happy prologues to the swelling act
> Of the imperial theme.

But the idea of the duality inherent in all things has rooted itself in his mind, and, turning aside, he debates to himself:

> This supernatural soliciting
> Cannot be ill, cannot be good.

Contradictory pairings, the foul and fair of things, are hard to decide between: if ill, one thing follows; if good, another, and he can only conclude his thoughts with a desperate abstraction which is a formula of the same inescapable duality – 'nothing is, but what is not'. The soldier has begun to speak the words of a metaphysician; it is as if the brain of Fortinbras had become possessed by the mind of Hamlet.

In Act I, scene iv Malcolm reports to the king the execution of Cawdor and remarks:

> He died
> As one that had been studied in his death
> To throw away the dearest thing he owed
> As 'twere a careless trifle.

This little speech introduces two themes: one, it hints at the idea of the worthlessness of existence, reducing life to a part to be studied (or rehearsed), anticipating Macbeth's 'poor player' in Act V, scene v; Cawdor executed, Macbeth is presented with his title and so he *becomes* Cawdor, stepping so to speak into his shadow and beginning at once to play the very same part, that of a murderous traitor who, by the time he comes to the same bloody end, will have the first Cawdor's dim and indifferent view of life. Macbeth, then, is two persons: the brave Macbeth is at internal war with the malevolent Cawdor, and his usurping the crown by murdering Duncan is an attempt to become superior to both the warring identities: it is an act of transcendence, a desire to become the authoritative *other* who will tolerate no rebellion from the schismatic adversaries within the body who claim an exclusive possession of the self. That Cawdor and Macbeth are closely linked as the foul and fair duality within the body of one man is subtly suggested by the second theme in the lines that follow. This is the theme of the false self that cannot be detected by outward appearance. Referring to Cawdor, Duncan says:

> There's no art
> To find the mind's construction in the face.

The generalisation made that expresses the theme, Duncan adds a particular remark about Cawdor:

> He was a gentleman on whom I built
> An absolute trust.

The very next words in the text are the stage direction: *Enter Macbeth . . .*, so that even as Duncan's words about having been deceived by Cawdor are being heard the audience watches Macbeth enter. Seeing him, Duncan greets him most warmly as 'O worthiest cousin': the words which he has been thinking he had been mistaken in applying to Cawdor become instantly attached to the person of Macbeth with the belief that this time the face does not mask a false self. The king has had a bitter experience with Cawdor, but does not learn a lesson. He had an 'absolute trust' in him and never knew that the trusting face he looked at was a traitor's. And when later in the scene Macbeth takes his leave, Duncan looks at him with very warm regard, as he must in order to say without the slightest intimation of irony, 'My worthy Cawdor!'

This theme of not knowing what one is looking at is connected with the *foul and fair* duality. It is also a knowledge quickly learned by Macbeth whose wife tells him in Act I, scene v:

> Your face, my Thane, is as a book where men
> May read strange matters.

and she teaches him to

> look like th' innocent flower,
> But be the serpent under't.

The lesson learned, Macbeth states it in its most memorable formulation, the line with which the curtain comes down on Act I:

> False face must hide what the false heart doth know.

But before this there is the dramatic scene of Lady Macbeth alone on the stage, appearing in the play for the first time, reading aloud her husband's letter:

> *They met me in the day of success; and I have learned by the perfect's report they have more in them than mortal knowledge.*

Macbeth surely means that the knowledge of the witches exceeds what can be known by ordinary humans, for they have a privileged perception of the future, which the latter do not. But the exquisitely ironical ambiguity exuding so delicately from the phrase, that the knowledge being forecast is of his own mortality, is lost on Macbeth; neither does he ponder another layer of ambiguity in the phrase, that because it unplugs the support system of belief that gives meaning to life therefore a knowledge of reality can be fatal when reality is seen to be a succession of perceptions that prove doubly illusory, each one being charged by the foul and fair duality.

Lady Macbeth does not pause to consider such philosophical niceties. She does not even question the nature of the witches. Unlike Banquo who on seeing the witches had wondered if he had lost his reason, Lady Macbeth reads about them as if they were no more than servants standing by the throne to help in her husband's coronation. She refers to them as 'metaphysical aid' with the same perfect understanding that such a thing exists and a generous measure of it is her due as a present-day leader talks of receiving 'foreign aid'. When she has read Macbeth's letter, she launches into her first soliloquy with an emphatic, no-nonsense declaration:

> Glamis thou art, and Cawdor, and shalt be
> What thou art promised.

Not only does she not pause to express amazement at the witches, she also does not stop a moment to wonder at the speed with which their first prophecy has come true, nor to express any satisfaction at her husband's new title. Of course, it is to the dramatist's purpose that he attend straight to the portrayal of her character and it is the triumph of his art that the first words he gives Lady Macbeth instantly capture her essential character. She is a person who admits no doubts and tolerates no opposition, so affirmative of her grasping determination is that phrase, *and shalt be*. Her words appear to be spoken with such uncompromising authority that when she proceeds, in the next nine lines, to analyse Macbeth's character ('It is too full o' th' milk of human kindness' and so on), the effect on the audience is both to believe that her analysis is accurate as well as to acquire an insight into her own character. She fears Macbeth's mild nature will not be up to the demands of their common ambition which she would prefer to win 'the nearest way', her conviction being that power must be ruthlessly grasped and not waited hopefully for, and in a wonderful revelation of her own strong sense of purpose she calls to him:

> Hie thee hither,
> That I may pour my spirits in thine ear
> And chastise with the valour of my tongue
> All that impedes thee . . .

No sooner does she make this wish when a messenger enters to inform her that the king is coming to be her guest and that Macbeth is soon to arrive. The verbal power with which she launches into her second soliloquy is explosive. Her first speech had been full of abstract words; she had wanted to inspire Macbeth to be ruthless in pursuit of the crown; but now, hearing of the king's imminent arrival, hardly has the messenger gone when she resolves the king must be murdered that very night and breaks into her second soliloquy in a sequence of terrifying and graphic images:

> The raven himself is hoarse
> That croaks the fatal entrance of Duncan
> Under my battlements.

She is fiercely opening the gates of hell, calling to the spirits, 'unsex me here' and 'make thick my blood' and appealing to them to

> Come to my woman's breasts
> And take my milk for gall, you murd'ring ministers . . .

and then in a climax of the evil thoughts pouring from her, she invokes darkness:

> Come, thick night,
> And pall thee in the dunnest smoke of hell,
> That my keen knife see not the wound it makes,
> Nor heaven peep through the blanket of the dark
> To cry 'Hold, hold!'

She is in an ecstasy of invocations to the evil spirits; she is prepared to make an offering of what is most vital and fruitful in her in exchange for unpitying force with which to attain her end; she is defying heavenly mercy.

Macbeth, the one who is 'too full o' th' milk of human kindness', enters and she, who has just made an offering of her milk in exchange for gall and implicitly put upon herself the curse of sterility, quickly instructs him on how he must assume a false face and 'Leave all the rest' to her.

The next scene (I, vi) is brief and seems to serve only to show that the king has arrived at Macbeth's castle where he is graciously received by Lady Macbeth with whom he exchanges polite courtesies, the obvious irony of which cannot be missed by the dullest among the audience. But not so obvious is the relevance of a remark made by Banquo at the beginning of the scene after the king declares he finds the air around the castle soothingly sweet. Banquo points to the martin which has a predilection for making its nest in several parts of the castle. His statement is the longest speech in the short scene and its language seems excessive, especially when he says

> No jutty, frieze,
> Buttress, nor coign of vantage, but this bird
> Hath made his pendent bed and procreant cradle.

The point of his extended reference seems only to be to express Banquo's nearly sycophantic agreement with the king, that the air is sweet around the castle, by alluding to the convenient example of the bird which has chosen the castle, thus proving that it is a place touched by 'heaven's breath'; and of course, since the echo still hangs in the air of Lady Macbeth's fiery invocation of evil spirits, the audience relishes the dramatic irony of the king and Banquo finding the castle as if it were situated in paradise. But there is a thought embedded in the bird imagery, and especially in the vivid, one could almost say pregnant, image of the 'procreant cradle', which is profoundly relevant to the play. For the martins, the castle is a wonderful place to build their nest and *to breed*. Banquo states about the birds:

> Where they most breed and haunt, I have observed
> The air is delicate.

So, nature itself is in agreement that Macbeth's castle is a blessed spot where creation flourishes. But we have just observed Lady Macbeth implicitly draw the curse of sterility upon herself; in the next scene we will be horrified to hear her say, in order to prove to Macbeth how ruthless she can be, that if she had a baby at her breast,

> I would, while it was smiling in my face,
> Have plucked my nipple from his boneless gums
> And dashed the brains out . . .

And it will be in the same castle, the same blessed spot chosen by the impartial birds where to breed and haunt, that she will go walking in her sleep, that she will literally haunt its halls. And Macbeth, whose mind conceives of pity as 'a naked new-born babe' in his soliloquy that opens Act I, scene vii, will become the murderer of children – and when Macduff is given news of the slaughter of his children, the phrase he will use in his intense grief will be 'all my pretty chickens'. And before that, in the scene in which Macduff's son is murdered (IV, ii), Macduff's wife, when told that her husband has fled, will use bird imagery with which to describe her situation:

> For the poor wren
> (The most diminutive of birds) will fight,
> Her young ones in her nest, against the owl.

Her son, asked how he will live without his father, replies, 'As birds do, mother'. When a messenger comes to tell her of the danger to her family, she asks, 'Whither should I fly?' And finally in this scene, when the murderer stabs the son, he accompanies his action with the words, 'What, you egg!' Though the mother is killed too, later, what we are shown is the killing of the child.

Lady Macbeth employs the image of doing brutal violence to a baby at her breast in order to put some resolve into her husband's wavering mind. The time has arrived for Macbeth to commit the foul murder but his mind is overcome by fair reason. Duncan has been so gentle and good a king that were he to be killed

> his virtues
> Will plead like angels, trumpet-tongued against
> The deep damnation of his taking-off;

it is a language that is a heavenly counterpoint to Lady Macbeth's hellish invocation. When she hears his doubt, which he expresses in the beautifully refulgent imagery of 'golden opinions', which ought to be worn like just-purchased clothes 'in their newest gloss', she flings against this luminous intrusion into her dark resolution a vituperative wall so thick that the sweet light of reason is quite shut out. She takes his conceit of the new clothes and turns it inside out: they will wear 'griefs' upon their faces to show their shock at the death of Duncan who will be seen to have been killed by his two chamberlains. Illusion will be presented as reality. 'Who dares receive it other . . .?' she asks triumphantly. Abandoning his doubts, Macbeth assumes the new, deceptive guise, and the first act of the play that had begun with the witches' mockery that 'Fair is foul, and foul is fair' ends neatly harmoniously in the summation of its theme with Macbeth proclaiming

> Away, and mock the time with fairest show;
> False face must hide what the false heart doth know.

*

The evil spirits have responded to Lady Macbeth's invocation; thick night has fallen upon the world. Enter into this darkness Banquo and his son Fleance, *with a torch before them* as if they would illuminate a true reality. And enter before them Macbeth with his newly assumed false face whose first words in Act II, answering Banquo's 'Who's there?', are a lie: 'A friend'. A servant, also *with a torch*, accompanies Macbeth, so that there is the mirrored doubling of the single image, the fair and the foul, truth and falsehood confronting each other, with long shadows of the players thrown across the stage, a visual representation that brilliantly projects a central conception of the whole drama in that brief moment's intense tension between Banquo's question and Macbeth's answer.

In his short dialogue with Banquo, Macbeth appears composed and very much in control of the mechanics of deceit which he has begun to manipulate with untruthful words. To Banquo he must seem his old soldiering friend. But the moment he is alone, Macbeth's hold over reality collapses. He is gripped by an hallucination. The dagger that springs before his eyes seems to have a palpable form but he cannot hold it. The language in which Macbeth questions the origin of his disturbing perception is also expressive of a philosophical analysis that states an *either/or* proposition in order to examine a fact claiming to be real:

> Art thou not, fatal vision, sensible
> To feeling as to sight? or art thou but

> A dagger of the mind, a false creation
> Proceeding from the heat-oppressèd brain?

The object has almost an empirically provable presence; only, it cannot be held. But it is not only a dagger that Macbeth is staring at, it is also a fatal vision that he has become possessed by. Of course, at the simple level the vision of the dagger is 'fatal' because the object is an instrument of murder; but the phrase 'fatal vision' stands out in Macbeth's desperate question with a portentousness that exceeds the simple metaphorical representation of an object. Vision itself, of which a dagger may be an example of an object that the mind may retain as an idea of empirically verifiable knowledge, could be fatal if it gives us not truth but 'a false creation', fatal because all delusion is lifeless, being merely the fantastic invention of an overwrought brain. Macbeth, the man of action who has recently won a battle, and thus defended physical territory, which is to say thus expressed his unquestioning belief in the existence of matter, is now gripped by doubt; progressively in the play, his actions become more intense and bloodier: like an addict who must ingest larger doses of the drug to have the original sensation, Macbeth's actions get increasingly vicious, as if he could regain his original belief in reality; also progressively, however, his distrust of reality increases until he rejects it altogether as signifying nothing. It is not cowardice that makes him hesitate – 'I dare do all that may become a man' he had said to his wife when she railed at him for not wishing to proceed with the murderous business. What stops him is something unknown to him within his own mind which has begun to lose hold over certainty, for if he cannot believe what he sees, then, as he acknowledges, his 'eyes are made the fools 'o th' other senses'. He shakes himself free of the hallucination just when the dagger has become so real it seems to have blood upon its hilt. Calmly he asserts, 'There's no such thing', and recovering control over his actions appeals to the world of solid substance:

> Thou sure and firm-set earth,
> Hear not my steps which way they walk, for fear
> Thy very stones prate of my whereabout . . .

After the murder has been committed, these words will find an ironical echo in Lennox's

> Some say the earth
> Was feverous and did shake.

And also by Birnam Wood that will come moving towards Macbeth. The earth will prove itself not to be firm-set at all, and will appear before his startled eyes as mockingly hallucinatory as the dagger. *There's no such thing*. Not only the dagger has no existence, but also there's no *such* thing because the world of objects could similarly be nothing but a complex of compelling images invented by the 'heat-oppressèd brain'.

Lady Macbeth comes to the stage just when Macbeth goes to murder Duncan. She has attended to the important details, such as drugging the grooms guarding the king and taking away their daggers with which the murder is to be committed. After Macbeth's soliloquy, her remark

> I laid their daggers ready –
> He could not miss 'em

is brilliantly ironical; indeed it would be almost comical were the situation not so dramatically tense. Macbeth returns, his hands bloodied with the deed, full of remorse, guilt, and the overwhelming thought that by committing the murder he has excluded himself from Christian redemption as well as corrupted the set purpose and order of nature. Where, just before the murder, he had talked about the sleeping mind as prey to unnatural forces and, absorbed in the surrealism of dreams, attracted to pagan ritual, after the deed he thinks of sleep as a restorative tonic, a condition in which anxiety is benignly suppressed and the disturbed being recovers as if he lay in a tension-relieving bath – a condition from which Macbeth must for ever be excluded. Nature's therapy and religious comfort can no longer be his. Aghast at her husband's words, Lady Macbeth advises him not 'to think/ So brainsickly of things', another remark which is nicely ironical, for it is Macbeth's having begun to conceive of reality – the world of things – as no longer 'firm-set', but unreliable and even illusory, that is causing his mind to become disturbed, giving him in the eyes of the practical-minded Lady Macbeth the appearance of a 'brainsickly' person. And the irony becomes even more subtle when one observes that it will be Lady Macbeth herself who will literally be afflicted by a sickness of the brain: Macbeth's lament about having lost for himself the great nourishment of sleep will be the disease in her mind which will make her haunt the castle without seeing any *thing* there. Macbeth has murdered sleep, and his corruption of nature infects the globe: were he to attempt to wash his bloody hand in the ocean, his hand would pollute the waters of the world.

The murder committed to possess the world more fully – and to have is to know, for intimate familiarity gives perception its presumptions about truth – Macbeth's vision should now be the unclouded one of the victorious warrior whose trophies are rich and ornate and, like those of Radames in Verdi's *Aida*, a wonder for all to behold; instead, Macbeth's bloody hand is empty and his vision from now to the end of his life will be beclouded by illusions so persistent in their mockery of the commonly held perceptions of truth that he will never fully know what it is that he possesses. And the language of the play, which established in the first act the images and ideas centred upon duality, paradox and hallucination, now begins to grow tentacles of ambiguity and cross-reference which wrapping their slippery limbs around Macbeth will gradually tighten their hold until he sees nothing. To be sure, *Macbeth* is a drama of ambition and greed; a play about character; a spectacle of blood and treason; but its profound fascination is at a deeper, unconscious level where all human beings struggle with an interior darkness: the more Macbeth acquires physical territory the less sure he is of what constitutes the true reality of physical matter.

The gate of the castle is the gate of hell, and the porter's language – '. . . it makes him, and it mars him; . . . it persuades him and disheartens him; . . .' – is an echo of *fair* and *foul*, with never any certainty of the thing possessing a single unambiguous identity. It is at this point in the play that the earth appears to have become feverous, and Macduff, as if he has come to the very heart of darkness, cries out

> O horror, horror, horror! Tongue nor heart
> Cannot conceive nor name thee!

There is the vision, certainly; he has seen it; but it cannot be known and there can be no language to describe it.

Pretending to be as spontaneously horrified as Macduff at the discovery of Duncan's murder and having heard Macduff add to his impassioned outburst the statement, 'Confusion now hath made his masterpiece', Macbeth forges a matching idea:

> . . . from this instant
> There's nothing serious in mortality:
> All is but toys.

Macbeth's attempt is to create a language that gives a false impression, making him appear as guiltless of Duncan's murder as Macduff; and surely, when he continues with the readymade consolatory cliché, 'The wine of life is drawn . . .', he is presenting himself as a grief-stricken friend; but his 'brainsickly' mind has uttered an idea that comes from his unconscious preoccupation with reality that will not hold itself still in one graspable and believable image but shows itself in mocking contradictions and confounding apparitions.

All is but toys. Four tiny monosyllables, and reality is dismissed!

The final scene in Act II seems constructed merely to further the plot, for from it we learn that Macbeth is about to be crowned and that Duncan's sons have fled and Macduff is going away to Fife. But the scene begins with an Old Man who makes the portentous statement that though in his seventy years he has seen 'dreadful' and 'strange' things

> this sore night
> Hath trifled former knowings.

Answering him, Ross uses an image central to the play, that of man as an actor upon the stage, and describes the contradictions in nature that he has witnessed: by the clock it should be bright day but the earth is gripped by night, and he has seen Duncan's beautiful horses turn wild and eat each other. The imagery is obviously calculated to arouse terror in the audience and to keep the dramatic tension at a high pitch; and when towards the end of the short scene Macduff refers to 'our old robes', it is also obvious that, as with Ross's 'bloody stage' and the Old Man's reference to birds, the playwright has begun to manipulate his imagery patterns in a compelling design, bringing closer to our perception the whole fabric of his thought. The scene of forty-one lines seems then to be a form of summary and a reminder; but the Old Man's opening remark, that what was formerly known has been belittled, is directing one's intellectual attention towards an idea different from the more graphic ideas claiming one's immediate absorption in the drama: one's conviction in what had been believed to be true has been overturned. The sun is *strangled* by night; which is to say, a shadow has fallen upon the universe. The darkened world, with its beasts and birds gone crazy, is a stage upon which is enacted Macbeth's interior drama. The Old Man's words with which the scene concludes, 'make good of bad, and friends of foes', once more re-states the *fair* and *foul* duality in a pairing of opposites that by now has become almost mechanical.

*

And if it had been forgotten that fair is foul, the very first sentence of the third act re-states the idea. Alone upon the stage, Banquo alludes to the fair that Macbeth has gained – 'Thou hast it now – King, Cawdor, Glamis, all,' – and, the stress demanded by the rhythm of his speech falling emphatically on *foully*, adds 'Thou play'dst most foully for't'. But after the Old Man's reference to the darkened world in the previous scene, the play has now begun to be perceived at a double level: there is the direct transmission of immediate matter, the living daily experience which, even though in this instance it is extraordinary, remains largely believable as a narration of uncommon events; but there is another drama that we have begun to witness, and that is the one taking place entirely within the universal shadow, in that immense darkness where the soul comes to confront the inconceivable and unnameable horror that Macduff had referred to after seeing the murdered Duncan: the drama that is interior to the person of Macbeth, the drama that transforms the story of a cold-blooded murderer and a brutal tyrant to a subconscious insight into the tormented mind's discovery of reality as a meaningless procession of generations from which the self receiving the sensations of experience and of history is excluded.

Consider the self, the *I*, trapped forever in the dimension of Time where it is exquisitely mocked each instant by time past and time future, consider the self with its feverish, anxiety-bound strategies with which to realise the dream of immortality, the winning of eternal Time. Shakespeare seems to have arrived at a Proustian solution early in his career, in his sonnets, where a future is to be secured not by gilded monuments but by a poet's art. It is a charming reverie that centuries hence the beloved's image will continue to breathe in printer's ink in some dog-eared paperback. But Shakespeare's later work, the tragedies especially, offer no such charming hope. In them, though there is always a Malcolm or a Fortinbras to continue the business of the living, time future is obliterated. When Macbeth says, 'There's nothing serious in mortality', he makes his declaration by first saying: 'from this instant'.

Time future is obliterated in Macbeth by his not having any heirs. When he plans the murder of Banquo, he remembers the witches' prophecy:

> They hailed him father to a line of kings.

But, he adds,

> Upon my head they placed a fruitless crown
> And put a barren sceptre in my gripe,
> Thence to be wrenched with an unlineal hand,
> No son of mine succeeding.

And when he goes again to the witches, desperately seeking a clue to the future which will re-instate him in the dimension of Time, he is shown a procession of future kings whose line is derived from Banquo who himself makes an appearance holding up a mirror and showing therein the infinite duplication of his own self. When the witches summon these apparitions of the past and the future, they do so reluctantly, having first told Macbeth 'Seek to know no more'; but compelled by his insistent 'Let me know', they meet his demand for knowledge and summon the apparitions by pointedly calling to them to 'Come like shadows'. The procession is of generations of humanity and it could continue in a future time that is eternal; but it contains nothing at all of the self which at this instant is the self of a man named Macbeth, that other shadow upon the stage, and the terror that fills one's imagination comes from the realisation not that it is Macbeth's fate to be killed but that his is a fate far worse: to become Time's outcast.

Macbeth conspires with murderers with the same motivation as a Mafia boss getting rid of the competition and covering his tracks by employing expendable hit-men. His conscience is not touched by remorse. He commits evil and remains unrepentant. Had he not been cut down by Macduff, he would have continued his barbaric tyranny, seeking out with his network of informers real and imagined enemies to murder. And yet we sympathise with him and are sorry for him!

Surely, our revulsion and shock at such acts as the murdering of Macduff's wife and children are great. If the language chronicled nothing but the bare facts of a tyrant's rise to power and the bloody force with which he maintained his evil rule, we would hold Macbeth in the same contempt in which we hold all the vicious dictators the world has known. But the language of the play is constantly undermining our direct, emotional response to the events being experienced by our senses by forcing into our intellect a subconscious awareness in which the mind's engagement is with abstractions that are temporal without being historical and of human consequence without being personal. When Ross comes to give the news to Macduff of his family's massacre (Act IV, scene iii), he says of Scotland

> Alas, poor country,
> Almost afraid to know itself. It cannot
> Be called our mother but our grave, where nothing
> But who knows nothing is once seen to smile;
> Where signs and groans, and shrieks that rent the air,
> Are made, not marked; where violent sorrow seems
> A modern ecstasy.

This is an image not so much of Scotland under Macbeth as that general image of universal suffering that has been projected by the imaginations of poets and artists throughout history – of which the most familiar example in poetry is Keats's

> The weariness, the fever, and the fret
> Here, where men sit and hear each other groan;
> Where palsy shakes a few, sad, last gray hairs,
> Where youth grows pale, and spectre-thin, and dies;

and a well-known example in art is Picasso's Guernica painting which, with its imagery of pain at the situation in which humanity finds itself, makes a strong impression even upon the minds of people who know nothing of Franco's Spain. Ross, wanting to prepare Macduff for the tragic news, says

> But I have words
> That would be howled out in the desert air,
> Where hearing should not latch them.

Though this statement is expressed in a form which is a conventional verbal formula for the conveying of profound personal grief, the language actually spoken is suggestive of ideas that transcend the immediate situation. It is a language that has echoed in the theatre from the time of Sophocles; the despair it alludes to concerns not only the poor unfortunate who has suffered a tragic fate, the allusion rather is to the idea of tragedy itself which is being suggested to the imagination as an inescapable human condition.

Of the two murderers whom Macbeth employs to attempt the killing of Banquo and his son, one has been beaten by 'the vile blows and buffets of the world' and the other is 'weary of disasters'. Here are two men from the lower depths, two shadowy figures from the underworld, surfacing briefly in the gloomy life-excluding castle to be sent out from there into the fading day where, one of them crying aloud 'A light, a light!', will bring a soul to its 'dark hour'; and yet the other says with more dignity than irony, 'We are men, my liege', and though the claim provokes a ten-line sarcastic comment from Macbeth the two do not have the appearance of criminal villains who can readily be hired for a hit job but rather have the demeanour of unfortunates whose days have been a succession of misery. They are not so much men who have chosen a career of crime as men whom desperation has made reckless. Though they function at a primitive level of brute existence, their quarrel, like Macbeth's, is with life.

Lady Macbeth is not tormented by those questions concerning existence that are unrelated to her own immediate well-being. She can generalise, as in Act III, scene ii (in rhyming couplets that sound remarkably like the dramatic verse of the future Dryden):

> Naught's had, all's spent,
> Where our desire is got without content.
> 'Tis safer to be that which we destroy
> Than by destruction dwell in doubtful joy.

Although her husband now has the crown, Banquo still lives and her happiness is incomplete. But her neat, jingling generalisation does not have the force to make the statement more than an utterance of a private anxiety. Her bland language is like the clearing of one's palate with a glass of mineral water before tasting the shockingly fiery pungency of what one must next swallow. 'What's done is done', she prosaically concludes one of her dullest speeches. Macbeth takes up the theme and his language transforms the idea which with her is one of personal lack of content to one of universal discontent. The speech which begins with the famous line, 'We have scotched the snake, not killed it', suddenly explodes with

> But let the frame of things disjoint, both the worlds suffer,
> Ere we shall eat our meal in fear, and sleep
> In the affliction of these terrible dreams
> That shake us nightly.

His wife is quick to observe that this is not how a kingdom-grabbing murderer is supposed to behave; nor is it how a monarch must appear before his subjects. She advises him to mask his 'rugged looks' and to present instead a 'bright and jovial' appearance among his guests that evening. Macbeth cries desperately:

> O, full of scorpions is my mind, dear wife!

It is a terrifying statement. Snake, scorpions. The snake's venom in one's blood, the scorpions' poison in the brain. Macbeth, the conquering soldier, has discovered another realm, that mysterious thing composed of body and mind, the self, but it is a realm which he cannot control, let alone rule, and must helplessly surrender to the poisons spontaneously generating themselves in that interior realm. But his words mean nothing to his wife who stares blankly at him and is, for once, nearly speechless, so that even when he tries to convey to her his plot to have Banquo and Fleance killed, he comments, 'Thou marvell'st at my words'.

Outside the castle: 'The west yet glimmers with some streaks of day'. The murderers are positioned to ambush Banquo and Fleance. Night is falling. Banquo is heard to call, 'Give us a light there, ho!' Shadows flicker upon the stage as Banquo and Fleance, the latter holding a torch, enter. A murderer shouts, 'A light, a light!' There is a confused movement of shadowy figures. Banquo is murdered. Just when Banquo falls dead, a murderer asks, 'Who did strike out the light?' Fleance escapes. The stage goes black, All shadows upon it become The Shadow.

Inside the castle, the banquet begins, and Macbeth is brought news of Banquo's death and Fleance's escape. Macbeth is seized by a fit, and the image of the snake comes to his mind again. The poisoned interior self rages against the reality that will not shape itself the way one wants to see it. Instead, reality presents the ultimate mockery to vision, hallucination: Banquo's ghost takes Macbeth's seat and thus not only does he symbolically dethrone Macbeth but also suggests to his perception that there is no distinction between the living and the dead. His wife's rational explanation, that

'When all's done,' he looks 'but on a stool', brings little relief to his disturbed mind, and the ghost comes a second time to intensify his torment. No command from Macbeth – 'Avaunt, and quit my sight! Let the earth hide thee!' – makes the ghost leave; he appeals to the ghost to take any other shape – bear, rhinoceros, or tiger – for a ferocious beast as his adversary would not so fill him with fear as does its corporeal representation of discarnate matter. The ghost does not budge until Macbeth shouts at it:

> Hence, horrible shadow!
> Unreal mock'ry, hence!

It is only, then, when he calls to the shadow to expel itself from his vision and, associating a conception of reality with the shadow, appeals to the mockery of reality to leave his sight, that he is released from the tormenting presence of the ghost. Assuming that such a darkened vision is not exclusively his, Macbeth is amazed that none of his guests is 'blanched with fear' as he himself is. Lady Macbeth prods the guests to leave without delay and without emotion, almost resignedly, hears her husband speak the words of his interior agitation – 'It will have blood, they say: blood will have blood' – and expresses no surprise when he changes the subject from a portentous pronouncement concerning the exposure of guilt to a calmly stated question about Macduff. But even as he talks about comparatively commonplace matters, Macbeth's language suggests ideas unrelated to ordinary events: he may wish to go to the weird sisters to have his future prophesied but to express his resolution as being 'bent to know / By the worst means the worst' is to seek a knowledge more powerfully illuminating. 'Strange things I have in head', he says, believing like all mortals that he has a complicated plan awaiting execution and not realising that his statement is also suggesting that mysterious phenomena possess his brain where things have indeed become strange.

It is a determined, a grimly resolute Macbeth who goes to the weird sisters and demands:

> I conjure you by that which you profess,
> Howe'er you come to know it, answer me.

The ten lines that follow in this speech are rhetorically powerful. Macbeth will brook no refusal. Even if the price of receiving an answer from the witches is universal destruction, he still demands to know it. The concluding, climactic figure in the sequence of images of destruction in the magnificently poetical language of this speech is to do with procreation:

> . . . though the treasure
> Of Nature's germains tumble all together
> Even till destruction sicken, answer me . . .

Macbeth is prepared to sacrifice the seeds of creation and to let Nature wither and turn to dust for the answer he seeks. It is the same ultimate rejection of life which Lady Macbeth had expressed when she had cried for the milk in her breasts to be replaced by gall. But the answers Macbeth receives from the succession of Apparitions summoned by the witches are riddles or metaphors – bits of language creating the illusion of communicating truth when what is understood is no more than an interpretation most appealing or consolatory to the listener. Encouraged by the information that 'none of woman born' can harm him and that he will not be vanquished until Birnam Wood moves to Dunsinane Hill, wanting one final confirmation of his own invincibility in the material world, Macbeth demands to know more: he asks whether Banquo's children will ever rule Scotland – which is to say, he asks about that future time when he himself will be no longer alive. The witches advise him: 'Seek to know no more'. He insists: 'Let me know'. This is when the witches, appearing to surrender to Macbeth's insistent command, make their final statement in the play:

> Show his eyes, and grieve his heart!
> Come like shadows, so depart!

Macbeth's pleasure in the earlier seeming prophecies is dissipated and he turns to immediate and practical business, crying, 'But no more sights!' He had asked to know, and what he has been finally shown is a future time from which his own self is excluded.

*

Malcolm paints himself most foully in Act IV, scene iii, proclaiming himself to be lecherous, avaricious and criminally lacking in 'king-becoming graces', and then rejects each graphically catalogued vice and makes himself to be the perfectly fair image of a virtuous virgin for whom truth and life are one. Before he astonishes Macduff with a shocking account of his vices, making himself out to be potentially a tyrant far worse than Macbeth and doing so probably to test Macduff's sincerity (for Macduff could have come to him as Macbeth's accomplice, and, being the son of the slain Duncan, Malcolm has every reason to be cautious), Malcolm first states his uncertainty about Macduff's allegiance, provoking him to declare, 'I am not treacherous'. To this declaration, Malcolm responds, 'That which you are, my thoughts cannot transpose', an answer that is nicely ambiguous; a line later, he adds:

> Though all things foul would wear the brows of grace,
> Yet grace must still look so.

The thought here is expressed very nearly as a proverb and is relevant to the play's core imagery which began in its first scene and will continue to its final minutes when Malcolm, the newly proclaimed king, will be surrounded by his 'kingdom's pearl' (among which pearls there surely will be a Cawdor and a Glamis, the first who had seemed to Malcolm's father a gentleman worthy of an 'absolute trust' and the other 'a peerless kinsman'). When Malcolm proceeds to talk of himself as a monstrously evil person, he illustrates the idea of a foul thing wearing 'the brows of grace'. Malcolm's foul self-portrait has been only a mask and when it is removed to show its opposite Macduff expresses his relief in a statement that could be a philosophical corollary to Malcolm's proverb-like utterance:

> Such welcome and unwelcome things at once
> 'Tis hard to reconcile.

Macduff's statement, emphasising the mysteriously contradictory ambiguity that is an inherent property of things or a cunning duplicity with which matter camouflages itself, concludes the idea with the sort of finality that indicates that what had begun in line 23 of the scene, with Malcolm's 'all things foul . . . the brows of grace', has been fully proved, and now, with Macduff's 'welcome and unwelcome things' in line 138, the idea is complete. That Macduff's statement puts a period, as it were, to a deliberately set out discussion of the idea is suggested by Malcolm's thoughtful response, 'Well, more anon', at which point a new character, a Doctor, enters the scene.

Why is Malcolm made to give such a long and graphic account of his imagined foul self? Act IV, scene iii is a crucial juncture in the play. Soon the curtain will rise on Act V with its rapid presentation of dramatic and bloody action. Earlier in Act IV, there have been strange apparitions and a murder. The third scene is in the nature of a pause, a momentary serenity before the explosive violence of the final act, and in it the author sums up or highlights the play's key images: the foul/fair duality, the unrelieved suffering which is seen to be the human condition, and the supernatural.

A dozen lines describe the remarkable power possessed by the King of England to effect a miracle cure upon people afflicted with scrofula (a disease also known as the king's evil). At first this might appear to have been put possibly to flatter the English monarch or to show a good king's attachment to his people to whom he is a healer, unlike a tyrant like Macbeth who is a killer of his people; but another, and perhaps a more significant, contrast is with the witches: the King has 'a heavenly gift of prophecy', unlike the weird sisters whose prophecies are malignant and the cause of death. The King's 'most miraculous work' cures people who are the 'despair of surgery', and his method is to hang upon the neck of the diseased a golden coin – 'Put on with holy prayers' – which superstitious invocation is essentially no different from the black magic of the weird sisters who, appearing to offer a cure to the diseased soul, metaphorically hang from the neck of the supplicant not a talisman but a curse.

The image of a helpless humanity seeking some desperate cure leads to the powerful projection of the image quoted earlier when Ross, come to convey to Macduff the news of his family's slaughter, describes Scotland as having become a universal grave and humanity can do nothing but fill the air with groans and shrieks. Though the information Ross has to convey concerns the murdering of Macduff's family, the message he brings is inexpressible:

> But I have words
> That would be howled out in the desert air,
> Where hearing should not latch them.

That he goes on to give the information – 'Your castle is surprised, your wife and babes / Savagely slaughtered' – in a direct, matter-of-fact language only heightens the imaginative power of the earlier statement. Human kind has learned to countenance the barbarity of tyrants and to endure inhuman suffering at the hands of a savage ruler; more chilling is the universal grief that is unrelated to a discernible physical cause, for his grief, associated with no adversary who inflicts the pain, is without cure. It is the pain that comes with knowing that one exists. It is mortal knowledge.

'You have known what you should not' says Lady Macbeth's doctor when he sees her walking in her sleep and hears her babbling fragments of guilty confession. Act V opens with this scene giving a vivid representation of the physically unharmed person who is stricken by a deep internal wound. Her eyes are open but, though she holds a taper in her hand and her shadow moves with her, she sees not the external world as she walks through the labyrinth of memory. Indeed, her real self is no more there than is her shadow. Her disease is incurable. 'More needs she the divine than the physician', says the doctor.

Macbeth re-appears in Act V, scene iii. He was last seen in Act IV, scene i when he had gone to consult the weird sisters and had been shown a future that excluded him and his final significant statement, a line before the end of the scene, was 'But no more sights!'. And now, when he re-appears, his first statement is, 'Bring me no more reports'. The reference is to the information about the English forces led against him by Malcolm and Macduff, but the words carry a more general suggestion: it is as if he no longer wished to receive knowledge and would rather block out the evidence of the senses. When he asks the doctor about the condition of his wife and is told of her disturbed mind, Macbeth's response is not just particular to his own situation but is the universal cry calling for an existence in which the self is relieved of that complex of torments which are the cause of unrelieved despair:

> Canst thou not minister to a mind diseased,
> Pluck from the memory a rooted sorrow,
> Raze out the written troubles of the brain,
> And with some sweet oblivious antidote
> Cleanse the stuffed bosom of that perilous stuff
> Which weighs upon the heart?

The *rooted sorrow* and the *perilous stuff* are more than the calamities and the wrongdoings, with their attendant guilt, of an individual life. Macbeth's cry rather is humanity's desperate appeal to be re-instated to that prelapsarian state where human innocence is uncorrupted by knowledge. But that cannot be, and when Macbeth shouts out, 'Throw physic to the dogs', the rage he expresses is against the inevitability of the physical body's organic degeneration and the impossibility of any restoration.

A short scene follows in which Malcolm arrives with his soldiers at Birnam Wood and commands each to cut down a bough and carry it before him. His language is interesting: 'Thereby shall we shadow / The numbers of our host . . .' *Shadow* is surely a curious word in this context (even though, if the sun is out, each man will be under a shadow), for clearly *disguise* or *confuse* would be more appropriate. But, of course, what is being represented here is the image itself of the universal shadow that will be seen to be physically creeping up upon Macbeth.

'A cry within of women', states the stage direction in the next scene, but there is no indication whether it is a cry of horror or a scream brought on by some sudden violence. Lady Macbeth has died – Malcolm later suggests that she took her own life 'by self and violent hands'. Macbeth is on the stage with his soldiers, preparing to go to battle, and remarks how indifferent he has become to fear, how horror no longer fills him with shock. News is brought him of his wife's death. And now comes one of the supreme moments in literature, the ten lines that begin, 'To-morrow, and to-morrow, and to-morrow', lines that drop a block of ice into the stomach of each individual in the audience, and, frozen in our seats, we hear, 'Out, out, brief candle!', remembering that the last person we saw with a candle was Lady Macbeth, and now here is all humanity reduced to 'a walking shadow' and all our grand conception of our being is nothing but

a tale
Told by an idiot, full of sound and fury,
Signifying nothing.

It is at that moment that a messenger arrives and informs Macbeth that Birnam Wood has begun to move. With the all-consuming shadow approaching, it is logical for Macbeth to say, 'I 'gin to be aweary of the sun'.

A Happy Ending

But now the women must be brought back to life and made the benevolent guardians of immortality, and we must all be charmed by chaste love and its attachment to a fertile future. The contemplation of reality has released the image of the overwhelming shadow, and so what can the poet do to distract himself from the unbearable finality of his tragic vision but turn to magical realism and construct fantasies of perpetual happiness? The male heroes are now a jealous old bunch, a morose lot composed of the likes of Leontes, Cymbeline and Prospero; the younger men, apart from the villainous rascals necessary for the plot, are, like Posthumus, incorruptible good chaps with little ambition than to raise a family; and the females are now young daughters whose innocent expectation of happiness is threatened by the embittered old men or by the young rascals.

There is the potential for terrible tragedy in *Pericles Prince of Tyre*, *Cymbeline*, *The Winter's Tale*, and *The Tempest*, and the poet, his mind apparently set on seeking a happy ending, goes beyond reality and summons a magical power to transform, or even transgress, reality, for the daughters must be protected from the catastrophe of male passions and the men must surrender the female's ultimate prerogative – to be the creator, and the custodian, of the future. Women who had been the first to die in the tragedies are now magically preserved as if in a time capsule from which they are released when the other elements necessary for the happy ending are in place: Thaisa remains sealed in Diana's temple for fourteen years in *Pericles*, time stops for sixteen years for Hermione in *The Winter's Tale*. Women have become indestructible, and even to be put in a chest and thrown into the ocean, as is Thaisa's fate, cannot kill them; the young, like Marina who becomes the property of a brothel, remain virgins until charming princes claim them as wives and take them off to some fruitful future filled with pink fat babies.

Virginity seems crucial to the being of these women. Imogen in *Cymbeline* who has married before the play begins is still a virgin when it ends. Her husband Posthumus says in his exile,

> Me of my lawful pleasure she restrained
> And prayed me oft forbearance –

which would suggest she had opportunities enough for consummation but preferred to remain, as Posthumus says, 'As chaste as unsunned snow', and will continue so until the circumstances are appropriate for her to accept her happiness. Hermione, viciously abused by her husband's unfounded suspicion, dies to the world, and is brought back miraculously – a statue is seen to come alive before the repentant Leontes' eyes – and stands before us as a chaste monument to marital fidelity. Her daughter Perdita, lost for sixteen years, can have but one suitable fate, to be discovered by the prince who will marry her. While even the older women like Paulina in *The Winter's Tale* are granted a husband in the happy ending, the poet lavishes his magical resources upon the young girls, plucking them out of dire situations and providing them with the ultimate happiness of their dreams. It's going to be a brave new world for Miranda.

In his late age the poet makes up dreams of happiness for young girls in flower who are at that stage of the bloom's perfect delicacy of skin and fragrance, and the body's ripe fullness after which it must decay if it does not reproduce itself, when the briefly arrested moment of the perfection of the flesh prompts in the male imagination a concept of ideal beauty, and the creative mind is enchanted into the belief that the dream it is inventing for another's reality could be a possible destiny for new pairings of the human species. It is almost as if the poet were young again when the audacity of his imagination had dispensed with reality altogether and had entered directly into the dream, stopping the flow of time at that perfect moment in the year when even the empty air is perfumed with sensual vitality, the midsummer night, and reality indeed is a dream. In the beginning were happy endings, before the light suffusing the stage began to fade and what was seen to be walking upon it was a shadow.